THE OTHER SON, THE OTHER BROTHER

THE OTHER SON, THE OTHER BROTHER

The Forgotten Life and Epic Times of
SAMUEL HARRISON SMITH

KENT DEAN

The Other Son, The Other Brother
First Edition

Sandy, Utah
Ponderthis.info

ISBN 979-8-9939573-1-9 (Paperback)
ISBN 979-8-9939573-0-2 (Hardback)
ISBN 979-8-9939573-2-6 (ebook)

Library of Congress Control Number: 2025924632

HIS036040 HISTORY / United States / 19th Century
REL046000 RELIGION / Christianity / Church of Jesus Christ of Latter-day Saints (Mormon)
BIO018000 BIOGRAPHY & AUTOBIOGRAPHY / Religious

Cover design: Sabrina Dean-Perry
Layout and formatting: Kaitlin Barwick
Editorial assistance: Steven P. Miller

꒳

To my wife Kalena,
the love of my life,
with whom
I have enjoyed life's journey

ACKNOWLEDGMENTS

I would be remiss if I did not acknowledge the valuable efforts of Jim Bernini and Stephanie Dean-Perry for their encouragement in reviewing and providing feedback on my original manuscript for this book. I am indebted to them.

CONTENTS

$\mathcal{P}$REFACE

Who was Samuel Harrison Smith? If you are familiar with the history of The Church of Jesus Christ of Latter-day Saints, you might remember that he was a brother of Joseph Smith Jr., the founder of the Latter-day Saint faith. You may have heard Samuel mentioned in a small anecdote or two regarding the early days of the church. Nonetheless, most people are not very familiar with Samuel Harrison Smith unless they have researched the Joseph and Lucy Mack Smith family and intentionally teased out Samuel's life story from the complex familial narrative dominated by the luminary presence of his brother Joseph.

Still, Samuel's life deserves our sustained attention. It is not exclusively a Latter-day Saint or religious story; it is an American story that reflects his ideals and struggles in the early days of the United States. Samuel Harrison Smith's life was about family bonds, friends and foes, love and hate, tragedy and victory, and murder and legacy. It is a story that may resonate with anyone, regardless of one's religious beliefs or lack thereof. Samuel's life might remind you of your own or your family's story.

In some respects, Samuel led a kind of Forrest Gump–like existence; he was randomly caught up in historically significant circumstances but overshadowed by family, friends, and events. Still, Samuel's life is much more than a historical footnote, and his story should not be relegated to obscure corners of Latter-day Saint history. He may have been the other son of Joseph and Lucy Mack Smith, and the other brother of Joseph Jr. and Hyrum Smith, but he led a life of consequence.

Samuel made a significant impact on his family and those around him. He shaped the historical development and narrative of The Church of Jesus Christ of Latter-day Saints. His story also represents a vibrant chapter to the voluminous narratives on life in the early days of the United States. Although entangled with his brother Joseph, his family, and the beginnings of the Latter-day Saint faith, Samuel lived his own life. The life of Samuel Harrison Smith is a story of family, faith, and the frontier. It truly is an American story.

PROLOGUE

Tunbridge

The mountainous and hilly terrain of Samuel's birthplace was densely wooded with beech, birch, maple, and pine trees.[1] A rich array of wildlife, including black bears, deer, moose, and rabbits, roamed this forested area.[2] A trout-rich river flowed through the woodland, winding for twenty-four miles before converging with other branches flowing eastward to ultimately serve as tributaries of the Connecticut River.[3] Around the banks of the First Branch of the White River, the foundation of a town was established in 1761 through a charter issued by the governor of the New Hampshire colony.[4] The town was named Tunbridge.

At the time, the colonies of New Hampshire and New York both were issuing town charters in order to lay claim to the land west of the Connecticut River. Tunbridge was just one of many town charters issued in the area by the two colonies. Ongoing land disputes caused confusion and unease among settlers, especially those who received land grants from New Hampshire. Settlers feared their land claims might be invalidated. As a result, residents united to form the Green Mountain Boys militia, led by Ethan Allen. A few years later, in 1777, they declared independence from Britain, New York, and New Hampshire by establishing the Republic of Vermont.

In 1791, the dispute between the Republic of Vermont, New York, and New Hampshire was resolved. Vermont was admitted as the fourteenth state in the newly formed United States of America.[5] In that same year, nearly five hundred people called Tunbridge, Vermont, their home.[6]

و

Early spring in Tunbridge brought moisture to the air, heightening the effect of the ongoing chilly temperatures throughout the handsome farms and pastureland scattered across the area's sloping valleys. One March 13, 1808, a small farmhouse was full of excitement and anticipation as Lucy Mack Smith gave birth to a son. She likely was surrounded during the birth by female relatives and neighbors, with one of the women most certainly serving as a midwife. Samuel Harrison was born, the fifth son and sixth child of Joseph and Lucy Mack Smith.[7] Lucy and Joseph named their newborn son after his paternal great-grandfather, making the infant the fifth male descendant of Robert Smith to bear this name.[8] Throughout his life, however, Samuel was sometimes just called Harrison.[9]

Tunbridge continued to develop. Its population had increased significantly since the town's founding nearly fifty years before Samuel was born. Around the time Samuel was born, over 1,600 people called Tunbridge home.[10] Tunbridge's growth mirrored that of the rest of the new nation. From 1760 to 1810, the population of the area that became the United States increased from under two million to over seven million.[11] About five years before Samuel's birth, the United States Senate approved the acquisition of the Louisiana Territory, a move promoted by President Thomas Jefferson. The land bought from France effectively doubled the size of the new nation.[12] The newly acquired territory encompassed land from the Mississippi River to the Rocky Mountains and from the Canadian border to the Gulf of Mexico.[13] Meriwether Lewis and William Clark completed their famous expedition in the new territory just two years before Samuel was born.[14]

Like Samuel's family, most Americans at the time lived on farms in small towns or villages.[15] As slavery was firmly established in the new country, most of the approximately one million enslaved people were concentrated in the South.[16] The United States that Samuel knew thus was primarily agrarian, with its major cities located overwhelmingly on the East Coast.[17] New York City boasted a population of nearly one hundred thousand in 1810.[18] Emigration to the young nation, mostly from Europe, continued and increased rapidly in the following decades. Still, a supermajority of the population consisted of farmers or persons otherwise intimately involved in agriculture.[19] Most food produced on farms was for the family or was sold in local markets.[20]

The Smith family followed this traditional occupational and economic template. Typically, families relied heavily on their children, even the young ones, to help maintain and sustain their farms. Boys as young as seven were taught farm work and performed a variety of farm chores.[21] From a young age, Samuel learned farming skills from his father and older brothers.

CHAPTER 1

Joseph and Lucy

Lucy's brother Stephen Mack moved to Tunbridge in 1793 and became a successful merchant there. The son of Solomon and Lydia Gates Mack from the Connecticut Colony, Stephen was the second-oldest son among eight siblings. The Mack family lived in Gilsum, New Hampshire, at that time, although Stephen's parents later purchased land along the border of Royalton and Sharon in Vermont.

Stephen loved Tunbridge and encouraged his youngest sibling, Lucy, to visit him in his new home. At that time, Lucy was mourning the recent deaths of her two older sisters, Lovina and Lovisa. Their deaths deeply affected her. In her melancholy, Lucy often felt that life was worthless. She sought comfort in religion. Lucy's mother had raised her in a devout and prayerful Christian environment, yet Lucy was not affiliated with any denomination. This left Lucy feeling spiritually restless. Perhaps to distract herself from her grief, Lucy eventually accepted her brother Stephen's invitation to visit Tunbridge. In 1794, she traveled to Tunbridge, located eighty miles up the Connecticut River from Gilsum.[1]

Three years earlier, in 1791, Asael Smith had purchased land in Tunbridge. Asael and his wife Mary Duty Smith were natives of the Massachusetts Bay Colony who lived in Topsfield,

Massachusetts. They had eleven children. Soon after buying land in Tunbridge, Asael sent his two oldest sons, Jesse and Joseph, to clear it. Then Asael and the rest of the family moved from Massachusetts to Tunbridge. Asael later was elected to serve as a selectman overseeing the town's affairs.

Earlier in his life, Asael was affiliated with a Congregationalist Church, but he eventually became skeptical of organized religion. He had grown interested in the theological views of Universalism before arriving in Tunbridge. Perhaps unsurprisingly, Asael organized a Universalist Society in Tunbridge. His sons Jesse and Joseph joined this group.[2]

Stephen Mack became acquainted with Asael Smith and his family, and it was through Stephen that Lucy met the Smiths. She described the Smith family as "worthy, respectable, amiable, and intelligent." During Lucy's second visit to Tunbridge, it soon became clear that she and Joseph Smith had more than just a passing interest in each other. On January 24, 1796, Lucy married Joseph in Tunbridge. Lucy was twenty years old; Joseph was twenty-four.[3]

CHAPTER 2

No Home amid a Religious Divide

The Tunbridge community played an important role in the early married life of Joseph and Lucy Mack Smith. Joseph inherited part of his father's farm, and Lucy and Joseph spent their first six years together there "tilling the earth for a livelihood." They soon faced tragedy. In 1797, an infant son was born and died. Despite their sorrow, they seemed rooted in the Tunbridge farming community. Lucy later gave birth to two sons there: Alvin, in 1798, and Hyrum, in 1800.[1]

In 1802, Joseph and Lucy moved to Randolph, Vermont, a town just seven miles west of Tunbridge. Although they had a stable life on their farm in Tunbridge, they were perhaps seeking to "advance their fortunes" through storekeeping. Lucy's brother Stephen may have inspired the decision. Joseph decided to rent out their farm while they lived in Randolph.[2]

Within six months of their move to Randolph, Lucy became seriously ill. A doctor told her he believed she had consumption. What was called "consumption" in the nineteenth century is generally considered to be tuberculosis today. Although Lucy's exact affliction remains uncertain, the death rate from tuberculosis was high at that time. Her mother Lydia cared for her "day and night with much anxiety." Deeply saddened, Joseph wept. While holding her hand and with tears welling in his eyes, he lamented, "Oh Lucy! My wife! You must die. The doctors have given you up, and all say you cannot live."

Despite this grim prognosis, Lucy was determined to survive. She "looked to the Lord and begged and pled" that her life would be spared, as she later explained, so that "I might bring up my children and comfort the heart of my husband." Lucy also said she "covenanted with God that if he would let me live, I would endeavor to get that religion that would enable me to serve him right." Then Lucy claimed a voice spoke to her, telling her, "Let your heart be comforted." Soon after, she began to recover and regain her strength.[3]

Meanwhile, Joseph's mercantile business was in debt, and his investment in ginseng root failed after he was cheated by an unscrupulous agent. These financial setbacks compelled Joseph and Lucy to move back to Tunbridge.[4]

During this time in Tunbridge, Lucy decided to attend Methodist meetings. Joseph accompanied her, despite his disbelief in the teachings of Methodism. When his father Asael and brother Jesse discovered the couple was attending Methodist meetings, they quickly expressed their displeasure. As a result, Joseph persuaded Lucy to stop attending the meetings. Lucy was "very much hurt by this," and she went to a nearby grove to pray for her husband. After retiring to bed that night, Lucy recalled, she had a dream. She interpreted the dream to mean that Joseph would accept the gospel "with his whole heart" when he was "more advanced in life."[5] Lucy's dream must have comforted her. If her interpretation of the dream was correct, Lucy and Joseph could live a joyful life serving the Lord and raising their family with a knowledge of His gospel. Lucy could not have known that, years later, one of her sons would also feel drawn toward Methodism.

After giving birth to their first daughter, Sophronia, they sold their Tunbridge farm to settle the debts they owed from their time in Randolph. Lucy later said that selling the farm was a "considerable trial" because it "deprived us at once not only of the comforts and conveniences of life, but also a home of any description." After selling the farm, the Smiths moved to the town of Royalton for a few months and then relocated to Sharon, also in Vermont, where they rented a farm from Lucy's father. Joseph worked on the farm in the summer and taught school in the winter, and their "circumstances gradually improved." About two and a half years later, in December 1805, Joseph Jr. was born. During the winter of 1807–08, Joseph and Lucy, who was pregnant, moved back to Tunbridge for a short time.

Samuel was born during this stay in Tunbridge. It appears the Smiths stayed with family during this period. Within two years, they moved again to Royalton, where their son Ephraim was born in 1810. Tragically, he died in infancy. A year later, their son William was born.[6]

CHAPTER 3

No Religious Home

Around this time, Joseph's "mind became much excited upon the subject of religion." Many years afterward, Joseph told Lucy that he had "visions" at night that convinced him that no religionist knew more than anyone else.[1] Joseph was influenced by the attitudes and ideas of the intellectual movement known as the Enlightenment, which pervaded eighteenth- and early nineteenth-century Europe and America. To be sure, Joseph was not highly educated and could not be described as an intellectual. Still, the essentials of Enlightenment thought and attitudes, although initiated and cultivated by the highly educated, eventually became embedded in the cultural fabric of everyday Americans through newspapers, pamphlets, and informal discussions across the new nation.

It seems clear that Joseph's critical thinking and skepticism about the religious establishment of his time were fostered by the powerful influence of Enlightenment ideals that had shaped the American cultural landscape over the previous century. Widely circulated pamphlets, such as *Common Sense* and *The Age of Reason* by Thomas Paine in the late eighteenth century, popularized Enlightenment ideas among the general population. Paine's writings in particular marshaled support for the American Revolution and nurtured skepticism toward traditional Christianity.[2] Joseph himself had a copy of *The Age of Reason*.[3] Thus, the Enlightenment ideals of individualism, skepticism, reason, and questioning political and religious authority were rooted in the populace.[4] Indeed, despite widespread belief in the Bible and Christian ideals generally, a supermajority did not belong to any denomination or congregation at that time.[5]

At the same time, Joseph clearly had an affinity for personal religious feeling and faith, especially as they related to Christianity, the Bible, and the realm of folk beliefs. Here, too, he was a person of his time and place. Despite the popularity of Enlightenment ideas regarding skepticism and challenges to institutional religion, a significant segment of the population continued to believe in personal religious experiences. Revivalism and emotional religiosity, as exemplified in the Second Great Awakening movement that began during this period, represented a backlash against efforts to eliminate miraculous and spiritual elements from religion. A significant percentage of Americans did not want religion to be purely an intellectual exercise of reason; they desired a spiritual, transcendental experience.

Joseph was raised with and embraced a Christian ethos which was unabashedly integrated with folk beliefs that fused Christian religion and magic. The revivalistic currents in America at the time dismissed "modern claims" of "visions and other spiritual gifts" as mere "magic."[6] This was a reaction to the reality that spirituality and magic were so often intertwined in early America. Thus, despite the efforts of many at the time to "make religion rational and to banish the miraculous . . . there remained . . . a strong current of belief in such things,"[7] as Joseph's interpretation of his night visions and religious excitement demonstrated. Joseph was not atypical in this regard, as "folk religion was the experience of 80–90 percent of Americans."[8] Alongside Lucy Mack's Christian and folk beliefs, Joseph certainly communicated and modeled this way of thinking with his children.

Furthermore, "beyond the widespread practice of folk magic . . . thousands of early Americans also participated in [the] occult [i.e., mysterious and esoteric] practices of treasure-digging."[9] During the time that Joseph Smith's family lived in Vermont, the state was somewhat of a "treasure-digging mecca."[10] His sons, including Samuel, would have been adept students of their father's beliefs. In retrospect, Joseph's night visions seemed to foreshadow the family's ultimate destiny.

CHAPTER 4

War, Division, Outrage

During this period, tensions between the United States and Great Britain escalated as the Napoleonic Wars engulfed Europe. Britain, seeking to control the Atlantic Ocean, threatened American maritime rights and trade with Europe, thus jeopardizing the larger American economy. In the end, Britain's unapologetic impressment of American sailors led the United States to declare war on it in 1812.[1] Samuel was only four years old at the time.

Alongside the Smiths, Americans closely followed the course of the war. Local newspapers and citizens widely debated the merits of war with Britain. Public sentiment was mixed. Citizens in Vermont and New Hampshire, where the Smith family resided during the war years, were divided on support of the war.[2] Overall, New Englanders generally opposed the war effort, while Westerners and Southerners tended to support it. The War of 1812, sometimes called the Second War of Independence, lasted nearly three years and effectively ended in a draw. However, only a small percentage of Americans participated directly in the war, as the United States did not enact a military draft. Instead of conscription, the United States relied on its small military, volunteers, and local militias as needed.[3]

None of the battles took place within Vermont or New Hampshire, where the Smith family lived throughout the war. As such, none of Samuel's immediate family served in the war; however, Samuel's uncle Stephen Mack did participate in the war effort.[4] Understandably, the American public was outraged when the British burned the Capitol building and the President's House (later officially called the White House) in Washington, DC. The Smith family surely was enraged as well. Samuel likely remembered hearing about the war and the burning of Washington, DC, as a boy.

CHAPTER 5

Can't Catch a Break

Not owning any property and seeking a more permanent home, the Smiths moved in 1811 from Royalton, Vermont, across the Connecticut River to Lebanon, New Hampshire, about twenty-five miles southeast. As they settled in Lebanon, Lucy recalled that they had "sufficiency to make us and our children perfectly comfortable." Katharine, Joseph and Lucy's second daughter, was born during this time.

In 1813, typhoid fever swept through Lebanon and the upper Connecticut Valley. Eventually, all the Smith children became sick, including Samuel. Joseph and Lucy endured extreme stress and anxiety as their children battled the epidemic. Eventually, all of their children appeared to recover from the disease. Joseph Jr. seemed to be recovering when he experienced pain in his shoulder. After weeks of pain, a doctor discovered a fever sore between his breast and shoulder. The doctor decided to lance it. Soon after, the younger Joseph began to experience pain and swelling in his leg. Several weeks later, a surgeon arrived and made an eight-inch incision between the knee and ankle that relieved the pain and swelling for some time. Soon, Joseph was experiencing more pain and swelling in his leg. Eventually, doctors recommended amputating his leg. Both Lucy and Joseph Jr. protested. Lucy asked Dr. Nathan

Smith if he could just cut out the diseased part of the bone to save her young son's leg. Dr. Smith agreed to attempt the experimental procedure. After the surgery and months of pain, Joseph Jr. recovered but had to use crutches for several years. The traumatic medical event left Joseph Jr. walking with a slight limp for the rest of his life. Samuel, about five years old at the time, must have remembered the extreme trauma and stress associated with his brother Joseph's medical ordeal.

The Smiths' financial situation worsened under the weight of the medical expenses they incurred during this time. Consequently, they moved across the Connecticut River to Norwich, Vermont, in 1814, where they rented a farm. Don Carlos, the eighth son of Joseph and Lucy, was born there in early 1816.[1]

Along with some of his siblings, Samuel probably attended public schools in Lebanon and Norwich at various times. Publicly funded neighborhood schools were common in these areas during that period. The usual age to begin public school was about five years old.[2] Popular textbooks in the New England region at that time included the *English Reader* by Lindley Murray and the *First Lines of Arithmetic*. Samuel and his siblings may have used these textbooks.[3]

After successive crop failures on the rented land in Norwich, including one in 1816 (the "year without a summer"), Joseph was determined to move. He had heard about fertile land in New York. By the end of the year, the Smith family would be heading to New York.[4]

CHAPTER 6

Palmyra It Is

Joseph eventually decided to move to Palmyra, New York. He set out for Palmyra ahead of his family. As planned, Lucy and her eight children, ranging in age from eight months to eighteen years, traveled with a Mr. Howard, who drove the wagon team to Palmyra. Samuel was eight years old at that time. The journey was expected to take three to four weeks.

Soon, Lucy realized that Mr. Howard was "an unprincipled, unfeeling wretch by the manner in which he handled my goods and money, as well as his treatment of my children." During a stop about twenty miles west of Utica, New York, when it appeared that Mr. Howard was about to leave with the wagon team but without them, Lucy confronted him. After publicly criticizing him in a barroom, she took the wagon and the team and left with her family towards Palmyra. Lucy described arriving in Palmyra with a "small portion of my effects, my babes, and two cents in money."

Regarding their reunion with Joseph, Lucy later expressed the "joy I felt in throwing myself and my children upon the care and affection of a tender husband and father doubly paid me for all I had suffered," with the "children surrounding their father, clinging to his neck, covering his face with tears and kisses that were heartily reciprocated by him."[1]

Surely, the events of the journey would have been seared into Samuel's young soul. The trial would help define his character and steely resolve.

The Smiths rented a home on Main Street in the village of Palmyra. To support themselves while getting settled, they sold refreshments at a small shop and goods from a cart during community events. Samuel likely contributed to these efforts, along with his brothers and sisters. Lucy also painted and sold oilcloth table coverings. Additionally, Joseph Sr., Alvin, and Hyrum worked as farmhands and performed odd jobs, including gardening and digging wells. About two years after arriving in Palmyra, Joseph and Lucy put money down on land in Manchester, around two miles south of Palmyra. Around 1818, Joseph and the older sons quickly built a cozy log home adjacent to the land along Stafford Road.[2] Samuel may have also assisted his father and older siblings in building this modest house. Years later, they finished building a larger frame house, which the Smith family moved into in 1825.

Religious revivals around the Palmyra area began in earnest in 1816, just as the Smith family arrived. The religious fervor in the area persisted for years. Revivalism became so widespread, and the evangelical "fire" burned so intensely throughout Western New York that it has become known as the "burned-over district" (a term popularized by the famous revivalist preacher Charles Grandison Finney).[3]

Joseph and Lucy raised their children in a devout Christian environment. Family prayer and Bible study were regular practices in their home. Although Joseph Sr. had reported many dreams with Christian undertones over the last decade or so, he was not inclined to join any specific church due to his earlier Universalist leanings. Still, Lucy longed for a religious home. Sometime after 1818, Lucy joined the Western Presbyterian Church in Palmyra. The Presbyterians had the largest congregation in Palmyra at that time. Likely influenced by their mother, Hyrum, Sophronia, and Samuel also joined the Presbyterian congregation.[4]

The religious divide within the Smith family would have been noticeable. While Lucy, Hyrum, Sophronia, and Samuel attended services at the Presbyterian church, Joseph, Alvin, Joseph Jr., and William seemed to avoid participating in Presbyterian meetings.[5] It is uncertain whether the youngest children, Katharine and Don Carlos, ever attended Presbyterian services, but there is no evidence they were ever baptized.

Young Samuel definitely experienced and understood the religious tension at home. Perhaps with his mother's comforting presence and guidance, Samuel's religious feelings, based on his young understanding of faith, grew more stable and gave him a sense of belonging as he regularly attended Presbyterian services in Palmyra. However, any feeling of belonging Samuel felt within the Presbyterian faith would not last long.

CHAPTER 7

A Vision

During this time, Samuel's brother Joseph was exploring his own religious journey. Accounts from that time indicate that Methodism was one of the paths Joseph was seriously considering. A resident of Palmyra said Joseph had a "spark of Methodism in the camp meeting." Another resident mentioned that Joseph joined a "probationary class of the Palmyra Methodist Church."[1] Joseph himself said that during his search he became "somewhat partial to the Methodist sect, and I felt some desire to be united with them."[2] As Joseph's brother William recalled years later, Reverend George Lane of the Methodist Church gave a sermon that influenced Joseph's desire to search the scriptures and pray about his unsettled religious questions.[3]

Reflective and determined, Joseph said he withdrew to a quiet spot in a grove next to his family's log home to pray. In his first known written account of his religious search and prayer, Joseph expressed concern for the "welfare of [his] Immortal Soul" and said he was "exceedingly distressed for [he became] convicted of [his] sins." He also said that "by searching the scriptures [he] found that mankind did not come unto the Lord but that they had apostatized from the true and living faith." At some point during his prayer, Joseph claimed, he saw

16

"a piller [*sic*] of fire light above the brightness of the sun at noon day come down from above and rested upon [him]," and he "saw the Lord and he spake unto [him] saying Joseph my son thy sins are forgiven thee."[4] Later accounts by Joseph provided additional details about this experience. Unsurprisingly, such a vision would have profoundly impacted him. As he later expressed, his "soul was filled with love and for many days I could rejoice with great Joy and the Lord was with me."[5]

Visionary accounts were quite common during this era and within the Palmyra/Manchester area, as many others "claimed visions of Deity."[6] Despite this rich spiritual environment among his community and within the Smith family, Samuel never claimed to have experienced a personal theophany. Perhaps he longed for such an experience, but Samuel most certainly respected his older brother Joseph's experience when Joseph shared it with him.

A few days after his vision, Joseph testified, he talked with one of the "Methodist preachers" and gave "him an account of the vision which I had had. I was greatly surprised at his behavior; he treated my communication not only lightly, but with great contempt."[7] It must have been confusing for Joseph to receive such a reaction to the visionary experience he had shared.

Despite sharing his experience with this preacher, it seems clear that for many years Joseph did not widely share or discuss what became known as his "First Vision." Neither the Smiths' neighbors nor the other residents of Palmyra and Manchester appeared to know about that vision.[8] Joseph's reluctance to widely share his vision would have been a natural reaction to the Methodist preacher's response to his story. Moreover, Joseph may have understood his vision as a deeply personal message received as he sought redemption for his soul. Even twenty years later, most who believed in Joseph's subsequent revelations and his role as a prophet appeared largely unaware of the First Vision.[9]

Initially, even Joseph's family members might not have known much, if anything, about his visionary experience. Joseph's account of his vision supports this idea. In his 1838 account of his First Vision (which was later included as scripture in the Pearl of Great Price, one of the four "standard" works of The Church of Jesus Christ of Latter-day Saints), Joseph states: "When the light had departed, I had no strength; but soon recovering in some degree, I went home. And as I leaned up to the fireplace, mother inquired what the matter was. I replied, 'Never mind, all is well—I am well enough off.' I then said to my mother, 'I have learned for myself that Presbyterianism is not true.'"[10]

Apparently, Joseph did not tell his family about his vision or how he discovered that Presbyterianism was not true, at least not on the day he said he received his vision. Nonetheless, decades later, two of Joseph's siblings, Katherine and William, both stated that they were aware of the vision he had *around* that time.[11] According to William, everyone in the family believed him. Decades later, William confirmed that "we all had the most implicit confidence in what he said. He was a truthful boy. That father and mother believed his report and suffered persecution for that belief, shows that he was truthful. . . . we never doubted his word for a minute."[12] Katherine asserted that a Methodist minister shared Joseph's story with other ministers, a move which increased the family's persecution and had a significant impact on their sister

Sophronia, who became ostracized from her peers, affecting her physical and emotional health.[13]

Samuel would have embraced his brother's visionary experience. It was later said that Samuel was "overwhelmed with awe" as he heard his brother Joseph recount the vision he had experienced.[14] Yet Samuel, like his sister Sophronia, may have felt marginalized to some degree within the Palmyra/Manchester community. Samuel later prayed for divine confirmation of the things that Joseph would tell him. Perhaps Joseph served as a role model in this regard.

Unbeknownst to Samuel and his family, the impact of Joseph's First Vision would profoundly affect the rest of their lives.

CHAPTER 8

The Allure of the West

After the United States' independence was reaffirmed with the resolution of the War of 1812, the new nation began to assert its interests more firmly, especially against European imperial powers. In 1823, President James Monroe issued a foreign policy statement known as the Monroe Doctrine. The Monroe Doctrine declared that the Western Hemisphere was a sphere of influence belonging to the United States and that any attempt by a European imperial power to control or oppress any nation within that sphere would be considered a hostile act. It was used to support US westward expansion and justify interference in political affairs within the Western Hemisphere.[1] Several US presidents, including Theodore Roosevelt, John F. Kennedy, and Ronald Reagan, have invoked the Monroe Doctrine.

The Monroe Doctrine was issued just over a decade before Samuel and his family moved westward to the frontier.

CHAPTER 9

Stones and Visions

Aside from the comfort and divine love he must have felt from such a visionary experience, Joseph did not change his daily life or routine. Rather, as he later stated, he "continued to pursue [his] common vocations."[1] Samuel, along with Hyrum, Joseph, and William, continued working the farm. The farm grew wheat and apples and produced maple sugar.[2] Around this time, Alvin, as the oldest son, appears to have taken a leading role in the family by, for example, hiring out his labor with his father to earn extra money outside of the farm.[3] Sophronia and Katharine probably helped their mother with various household chores and caring for young Don Carlos.

In July 1821, Joseph Smith Sr. and Lucy Mack welcomed their last child, a daughter named Lucy. She was born in their small, relatively new log home near Manchester. The modest 1,000 sq. ft. house must have felt even smaller with Lucy's arrival. To create more space for the growing family, a bedroom was added at the back of the home.[4] Samuel, who was thirteen at the time, was the middle child. While learning from his older siblings, Samuel also took on the role of an older brother to his younger brothers and sisters.

It was not long before Hyrum and Joseph Jr. joined their father and Alvin in hiring out their labor at various times.

This would have increased Samuel's responsibility in helping to maintain the Smith farm. However, at times, Samuel also helped his father or brothers as a hired hand away from the family farm.[5] Sometime in 1822, Alvin began work on a larger frame house for the family near their log home.[6] "I am going to have a nice, pleasant room for father and mother to sit in, and everything arranged for their comfort. They shall not work any more as they have done," Alvin is quoted as saying.[7]

Sometime in 1822, a neighbor named Willard Chase hired Alvin and Joseph Jr. to help him dig a well. While digging, they found a small, dark stone. Chase described it as a "curiosity." According to Mr. Chase's later statement, Joseph borrowed the stone from him.[8] His mother later said that Joseph could see things through the stone that were "invisible to the natural eye."[9] Most likely, Samuel and his other siblings saw and handled the stone. They may have also seen Joseph Jr. use it to find "hidden" things. Undoubtedly, Samuel believed in Joseph's abilities with it.

As the use of physical objects for supernatural or spiritual purposes seemed to mirror some biblical practices, "peep stones or pebbles" and "mineral rods" were often employed to locate buried treasures or lost items.[10] The Smith boys, including Samuel, sometimes worked to find buried treasures. As a Palmyra resident recalled decades later, "There was considerable digging for money in our neighborhood by men, women, and children." Additionally, a nearby resident in Palmyra claimed he talked with Joseph Sr. and "learned, from his own lips, [that the elder Smith] was a firm believer in witchcraft and other supernatural things; and had brought up his family in the same belief."[11]

In late September 1823, about three and a half years after his First Vision, as Joseph Jr. recalled, he retired to bed one evening on the upper level of their log home. He said he "betook [himself] to prayer and supplication to the Almighty God for forgiveness of all [his] sins and follies, and also for a manifestation to [him], that [he] might know of [his] state and standing before him; for [he] had full confidence in obtaining a divine manifestation, as [he] previously had one."[12] According to Joseph Jr., "While [he] was thus in the act of calling upon God, [he] discovered a light appearing in [his] room," and a "personage appeared at [his] bedside." Joseph said the personage "said unto [him] that he was a messenger" whose "name was Moroni" and who declared "that God had a work for [him] to do."

In his 1838 account of this visit, Joseph stated that Moroni told him of a book written on gold plates and "two stones in silver bows" fastened to a "breastplate" but said that when Joseph was to receive these items, he should not show them to anybody. Joseph stated that his mind was opened to understand where the plates and related items were hidden. He remembered the messenger appearing two more times that evening and that his encounters lasted "the whole of that night."[13] Although Joseph shared his bedroom with his brothers, including Samuel, none of them woke up during his experience with Moroni.

The next morning, Joseph went to work with his father but felt "exhausted." Joseph Sr., noticing his son's fatigue, told him to go home. As Joseph Jr. started home, crossing a fence, he fell and lost consciousness. Then, he remembered, the same messenger appeared again and related everything he had told him during the night. As directed by the messenger, Joseph returned to his father and described his experience. His father believed him and advised him to follow the messenger's instructions.

Immediately, Joseph went to the hill not far from his log home where the plates and other items were buried. Joseph said that he "knew the place the instant that I arrived there." The items were buried on the west side of the hill, not far from the hilltop, and beneath a large stone. By removing dirt from the edges of the stone and perhaps by using a tree branch as a lever, Joseph lifted the stone and claimed to see the items just as the messenger had described them. As he recounted in his 1838 account, the messenger forbade him from taking the items at that time and instructed him to meet the messenger every year there for the next four years.[14]

Unlike his First Vision experience, Joseph told his father about his encounters with Moroni shortly after they happened, as instructed. Joseph Jr. also shared the same with the rest of the family that same day. If Samuel was amazed by Joseph's first visionary experience, he must have been awe-struck by Joseph's story of meeting Moroni. Furthermore, Joseph's account of the buried gold plates and stones seemed consistent with their family's treasure-seeking efforts and activities.

For the Smith family, Joseph's story of Moroni's visit most certainly foreshadowed something important. Years later, Lucy recalled that during this time "the sweetest union and happiness pervaded our house. No jar nor discord disturbed our peace, and tranquility reigned in our midst." Lucy also said that during evening conversations around that time Joseph would "describe the ancient inhabitants of this continent, their dress, their manner of traveling, the animals which they rode, the cities that they built, and the structure of their buildings with every particular, their mode of warfare, and their

24

religious worship as specifically as though he had spent his life with them."[15] No doubt, Samuel was enchanted by what Joseph shared with him and his family.

CHAPTER 10

A Death

In November 1823, Alvin fell ill with "bilious colic." A doctor came to the Smith home and administered a heavy dose of calomel. The calomel "lodged in his upper bowels," and Alvin's health quickly worsened. Knowing death was near, Alvin talked individually with each of his siblings. He specifically told Joseph to "do everything that lies in [his] power to obtain the [gold] record" and to "be faithful in receiving instruction and in keeping every commandment that is given."[1] There is no record of what Alvin told Samuel. Certainly, Alvin's words to Samuel would have been cherished by him throughout his life. Alvin died within days. An autopsy seemed to confirm that Alvin's death was caused by the calomel lodged in his bowels.[2] Alvin was soon buried in the Palmyra village cemetery.

The death exacted a tremendous emotional toll on the family. The impact on Samuel must have been strong. At age fifteen, he experienced a loss unlike any he had known, and it was undoubtedly deeply sobering. Lucy later said, "We were for a time almost swallowed up in grief, so much so that it seemed impossible for us to interest ourselves at all about the concerns of life. The feeling of every heart was to make speedy preparation to follow him who had been too much the idol of our hearts."[3] Alvin was unquestionably the favored son. As

Lucy implied when she said Alvin was "the idol of our hearts," Samuel looked up to Alvin as a role model.

On top of the family's deep grief, Alvin's death adversely affected the family's financial situation. Additionally, the larger house Alvin had begun building for the family the year before remained unfinished. Samuel's work and productivity on the family farm became even more vital. Samuel's father was over fifty years old at that time, and Joseph Sr. later admitted that he had "not always set that example before my family that I ought" and at times had been "out of the way through wine." Alvin seemed to have acted as an "auxiliary family head" in the years before his death.[4] Although there is no evidence that Joseph Sr. drank excessively when considering the broader historical context, he later regretted not being the husband and father he wanted to be then. While Samuel still had two older brothers (Hyrum and Joseph), the loss of Alvin and his father's perceived and actual shortcomings must have weighed heavily on him and shaped his early life in rather difficult terms.

CHAPTER 11

Work and Marriage in the Family

About two years after Alvin's death, the Smiths' large frame house was completed. With the Smith boys busy maintaining a productive farm and Joseph Sr. nearing age fifty-five, the family hired a neighbor, Russell Stoddard, to finish the construction.[1] The Smiths eagerly moved into the newly built house, where they enjoyed a more spacious and comfortable living environment. Joseph Sr., Lucy, Samuel, and his siblings were undoubtedly pleased by the additional rooms in their new home.

The Smiths received an opportunity to earn extra income in the fall of 1825. Mr. Josiah Stowell of South Bainbridge visited the Smiths to hire them to search for a silver mine near Harmony, Pennsylvania. Harmony was about 135 miles southwest of Palmyra. Previously, Stowell had met the Smiths while purchasing their wheat in the Palmyra area. Stowell understood that Joseph Jr. "was in possession of certain means, by which he could discern things, that could not be seen by the natural eye."[2] Stowell had heard some version of the story circulating in the Palmyra area about the small dark stone found while digging a well at the Willard Chase home a few years earlier and Joseph's use of the stone. By November, Joseph Sr. and Joseph Jr. agreed to Stowell's employment offer. During their absence, Hyrum and Samuel would have taken a leading role in maintaining the farm.

While boarding at Isaac Hale's home in Harmony, Pennsylvania, during the Stowell digging expedition, Joseph Jr. met Emma, Isaac Hale's daughter. Emma caught Joseph's attention. Although no silver was found during the weeks-long digging expedition, Joseph discovered a different treasure.[3] Joseph naturally would have told his family about his interest in Emma Hale.

Sometime in early 1826, a relative of Josiah Stowell filed charges against Joseph Jr., accusing him of being a disorderly person and an impostor. This relative was concerned about Joseph's undue influence over Stowell. A court hearing was held in South Bainbridge in March 1826. Stowell himself and others testified at the hearing that Joseph was not guilty of the charges. Due to the limited historical records and differing witness accounts, it is unclear exactly what the court ultimately decided. What is certain is that the hearing did not result in any significant charges or convictions.[4] Joseph's parents and siblings must have been shocked that such a charge was even made. To the Smith family, it was Stowell who recruited Joseph Jr. to work on the digging expedition.

In less than a year, both Hyrum and Joseph were married. In November, Hyrum married Jerusha Barden and moved into the small log home his family had vacated. About two months later, in January 1827, Joseph and Emma eloped and moved in with the Smith family at the large frame house.[5] That fall, Hyrum and Jerusha's first child arrived. They named their newborn daughter Lovina.[6] She became the first grandchild in the Smith family and was surrounded by loving uncles and aunts. More grandchildren were forthcoming.

Samuel quickly became the indispensable son of the family. By that time, Samuel was nearly nineteen years old. Described as six feet tall, athletic, and endowed with "great strength exceeding that of an ordinary man, enabling him to do an unusual amount of work," his farm labor and family contributions were valued by his parents and siblings.[7] Still, during his quieter moments, with Alvin's passing and the marriages of Hyrum and Joseph, Samuel must have wondered what life had in store for him in the coming years.

CHAPTER 12

The Plates and Trouble

Josiah Stowell and Joseph Knight, a farmer from Colesville who had earlier hired Joseph Jr. as a farmhand, were guests at the Smith home in the fall of 1827. They arrived on September 20 and stayed for two nights. Just after midnight, in the first minutes of September 22, Joseph and Emma prepared to leave. Lucy saw Emma with her "bonnet and riding dress" just before their departure. Joseph and Emma used Joseph Knight's horse and wagon for their stealthy nocturnal outing.

Joseph was focused on his objective. He knew exactly where he was headed. Joseph needed to go that day, as instructed, to get the gold plates. Rumors about Joseph finding gold plates had circulated in Palmyra and Manchester. He was certain he would be watched closely. Retrieving the plates in the darkness in the early morning seemed the best plan. Lucy knew where Joseph and Emma were headed. Anxious, Lucy found that sleep was not forthcoming. Before she knew it, dawn was breaking. Lucy knew Joseph and Emma had not yet returned. Worried about them, she went to the kitchen to start breakfast for her family and guests.

Soon after the family and guests arose, Joseph and Emma returned.[1] Joseph told his mother he had retrieved the plates, but they were not with him. He said he had hidden the plates in an old birch log not far from the Smith home. Soon, everyone in the family knew Joseph had retrieved and hidden the plates. Samuel was probably excited, thinking his brother had found and obtained the gold plates through supernatural means. A few days later, Joseph recalled, he retrieved the plates from the birch log. He brought them home hidden in his frock. After placing them in a small wooden box, Joseph hid the box under the hearthstones in the west room of the house.

Soon after, the Smiths noticed an armed group of men approaching their home. They quickly devised a plan to face the impending danger. Samuel, along with his parents and siblings, likely felt apprehensive. As the armed men drew near the Smith house, Joseph Jr. quickly carried out the improvised plan. Joseph, Joseph Sr., Hyrum, William, Samuel, and eleven-year-old Don Carlos rushed out the door, shouting to surprise and disorient the approaching men. The tactic worked. The armed group, apparently thinking a large number of men had come out of the house to attack them, quickly dispersed and did not return. The Smiths must have been relieved that they had frightened the armed band. They maybe even chuckled a little.

A few days later, Joseph recalled, he removed the plates from the hearthstones, wrapped them in clothes, and hid them in the loft among some flax in Joseph Sr.'s cooper shop just south of their apple orchard. The next morning, the Smiths found the shop in disarray. A group linked to Willard Chase had entered the cooper shop the previous night searching for the plates. The group failed to locate them.[2]

Some contemporaries of Joseph Smith and many later writers have argued that the gold plates never existed. It is probably impossible to determine how many people who knew Joseph and the Smith family believed that Joseph never found or possessed any gold plates. However, it seems that most people living in Palmyra and nearby areas who personally knew the Smiths initially thought Joseph had gold plates of some kind. There is documentary evidence that some neighbors of the Smiths who never became religiously involved with Joseph appeared to believe that he had gold plates.[3] Additionally, if Willard Chase or others did not believe Joseph had gold plates, it seems unlikely that he or others would have invested effort in trying to find and take possession of them by surreptitiously entering and ransacking the Smiths' cooper shop. Members of Joseph's family consistently maintained the existence of the plates throughout their lives, even decades later; that group included those who later left the church or any of the related religious movements Joseph inspired. Furthermore, eleven people later claimed to have seen the gold plates and held that belief throughout their lives; that list includes persons who eventually disavowed Joseph. Some writers have claimed that at least some of these eleven witnesses eventually retracted their claims about the plates or questioned the credibility of the plates. Nevertheless, most such arguments weaken under historical scrutiny or are challenged by scholars within the Latter-day Saint community.[4] Critics contend that the plates' existence is doubtful because Joseph did not allow them to be widely examined. Believers argue that witnesses saw the plates and that there is no other plausible explanation for the resulting text or translation.

Amid the turmoil over the plates, Joseph felt it was necessary to leave Palmyra to translate the writing on the gold plates into English. In November, after Joseph and Emma received an invitation from Joseph's father-in-law Isaac Hale, Emma's brother Alva Hale brought a horse and wagon to help relocate them to Harmony, Pennsylvania. Harmony was a small town with just over three hundred residents at the time. Before Joseph left, family friend Martin Harris, a wealthy Palmyra farmer, gave Joseph fifty dollars to help him settle in Harmony. Reportedly, Joseph placed the plates in a wooden box, which was then hidden in a barrel of beans and loaded onto Alva's wagon. Alva, Joseph, and Emma arrived in Harmony in December. The farmhouse the newlyweds moved into was built by Emma's brother Jesse fourteen years earlier and was located just a few hundred yards from the wide, shallow waters of the Susquehanna River.[5]

With Joseph's move, Samuel's responsibilities on the Smith farm increased. In early December, Sophronia married Calvin Stoddard.[6] All of Samuel's older siblings were now married. As the oldest sibling living at home, Samuel's family role naturally changed as his younger brothers and sisters looked to him for guidance. With Sophronia moving a few miles away from the Smith home, additional responsibilities fell on Katharine and Lucy to help their mother manage the household.

CHAPTER 13

Martin: A Question of Character(s) and Loss

Soon afterward, Martin Harris visited Joseph in Harmony. One early account of Harris's visit with Joseph states that Harris claimed the Lord told him he was to take some of the characters from the plates to New York City.[1] Apparently, Joseph agreed to the endeavor. After obtaining a copy of some of the characters from the gold plates, Martin Harris showed them to, among others, Professor Charles Anthon of Columbia College in February 1828. According to Harris, Anthon confirmed the characters were "Egyptian, Chaldaic, Assyriac and Arabic" and that they were "true characters." Professor Anthon later denied authenticating the characters. However, it was clear that Martin Harris did meet with Anthon, and Harris was more convinced than ever of the authenticity of the gold plates.[2]

For months, Emma served as Joseph's scribe, translating the gold plates into English. Then, in April 1828, Martin Harris returned to Harmony and served as Joseph's scribe for about two months. By that time, 116 pages of the manuscript had been completed. Harris obtained Joseph's approval to take the manuscript to New York to show his wife and some relatives. Weeks later, Harris confessed to Joseph that he had lost the manuscript. Harris was distraught, telling Joseph, "Oh! I have lost my soul." The Smith family was devastated by this news. It would have been natural for them to worry about possible severe divine consequences. Joseph claimed, through divine revelation, that he was not to retranslate the lost manuscript, and said that he received divine chastisement for the entire episode.[3]

Just after Martin Harris left for Palmyra with the manuscript, Emma gave birth to a boy. The infant died shortly after birth. They named their son Alvin in honor of Joseph's oldest brother. Emma was also gravely ill but recovered within a few weeks.[4]

Soon, Joseph recalled, he began receiving revelations from God to guide himself and others, including Samuel.

CHAPTER 14

A Convert

In late 1828, a young man named Oliver Cowdery was hired as a schoolteacher in the Manchester district. Eventually, he boarded with the Smith family. Through rumors in the area and information from the Smith family, Cowdery learned about Joseph and the plates.[1] Cowdery's stay at the Smith home seems to have roughly coincided with Lucy, Hyrum, and Samuel's disinterest in worshipping with the Western Presbyterian Church.[2] It seems Joseph's work with the plates began to change their religious feelings.

Sometime in March 1829, Cowdery was determined to visit Joseph Jr. in Harmony and told Lucy: "I have resolved what I will do . . . [what seems to be] working in my very bones insomuch that I cannot for a moment get rid of it. . . . I have made it a subject of prayer . . . and I firmly believe that it is the will of the Lord that I should go. If there is a work for me to do in this thing, I am determined to attend to it."[3]

In April, Cowdery traveled to Harmony with Samuel. The long trip was especially challenging because of inclement weather. When they arrived in Harmony, Samuel introduced Cowdery to Joseph; it was the first time Joseph Jr. had met Cowdery. Within a few days, Cowdery began serving as Joseph's scribe. Now that Cowdery was there, Samuel stayed for a while to help with Joseph and Emma's farm. On earlier trips to Harmony, Samuel had also served as Joseph's scribe. Samuel was always willing to help wherever he was needed.

Most of the translation of the plates appears to have been done while Samuel was in Harmony working on his brother's farm.[4] Before Samuel and Cowdery arrived in Harmony, Joseph's work on the translation had slowed down considerably, as Emma's household duties consumed so much time that she could rarely serve as her husband's scribe.[5] Undoubtedly, without Samuel taking Cowdery to Harmony and working extensively on his brother's farm, the translation would not have advanced so quickly during that time (and might not have progressed at all). It is possible that the history and final publication of the plate's contents would have been very different without Samuel's support.

During the translation, according to their accounts, some passages from the plates prompted Joseph and Cowdery to pray about the authority to baptize. Finding a secluded spot in the woods near Joseph's farm in Harmony, they prayed. Joseph and Cowdery claimed that during their prayer a messenger from God appeared and "laid his hands upon us [and] he ordained us" to the Aaronic Priesthood. The messenger identified himself as John the Baptist and instructed them to baptize each other. According to their statements, Joseph and Cowdery quickly baptized each other in the nearby Susquehanna River. They also asserted that they later received the Melchizedek Priesthood from the New Testament apostles Peter, James, and John somewhere along the banks of the Susquehanna River.[6]

Around this time, the Smith family in Manchester was forced to leave their large frame house because they could no longer afford to keep up payments on the farm. However, they were allowed to rent the small log home they had built a few years earlier. This was a significant loss for the Smith family. With such a large family, the Smiths would have to live uncomfortably in the log home for the rest of their time in the Palmyra/Manchester area.[7]

Samuel again visited Harmony in late May. Joseph told Samuel that the fullness of the gospel was about to be revealed anew and that priesthood authority had been restored. As such, the underpinnings of Joseph's theophany resembled those of Restorationist movements that had developed in early nineteenth-century America. Joseph also showed Samuel what had been translated. Although Samuel loved and admired his brother, Samuel was not "easily persuaded of these things," as Joseph later acknowledged.[8] He was his own man. Samuel believed the translation of the plates would spark a reformation among the existing churches. He did not expect Joseph to be baptizing converts or organizing a new church.[9]

Perhaps recalling his brother Joseph's experience, Samuel withdrew to the woods to pray. When he returned, Samuel was convinced that Joseph was telling the truth and asked to be baptized. Oliver baptized Samuel in the Susquehanna River just ten days after Cowdery himself had been baptized.[10] Thus, Samuel became the third person baptized in this new religious movement.

Samuel's conversion and baptism foreshadowed events that would soon unfold within the Smith family and among those connected with the Smiths. Samuel's life was forever changed as he immersed himself in his brother's religious movement.

CHAPTER 15

I Saw Them!

Rumors that Joseph was translating the plates at his Harmony farm increased the pressure on him to move again. Cowdery wrote to his friend David Whitmer to ask if Joseph could finish the translation at the Whitmer family's hundred-acre farm in Fayette, New York.[1] Fayette was a scenic town with about 3,200 residents nestled between the finger lakes of Lake Seneca and Lake Cayuga.[2] It was located roughly thirty miles southeast of Palmyra. David Whitmer and his family were connected to the Reformed Church in the Fayette area. David's father, Peter, was described by contemporaries as an honest, highly respected, God-fearing, and industrious German farmer.[3] In June, David Whitmer arrived in Harmony to help Joseph and Cowdery move to his family's Fayette home. Emma stayed in Harmony for the moment. Several weeks later, Joseph finished the translation of the plates in Fayette.[4]

Then, on June 28, according to their accounts, Joseph, Oliver Cowdery, David Whitmer, and Martin Harris went into the woods near the Whitmer farm. They returned claiming that an angel had shown them the plates and that they were commanded to testify of their truth.[5] A statement to that effect was composed in what seems to be Oliver Cowdery's handwriting.[6]

A few days later, in Manchester, Joseph showed the plates to eight people, according to their statements. Their statements claim that the plates shown to them had "the appearance of gold" and that "we did handle [them] with our hands; and we also saw the engravings thereon, which has the appearance of ancient work, and of curious workmanship," for "we have seen and hefted, and know of a surety." Samuel was one of those eight. Five of the eight men were part of the Whitmer family: Christian Whitmer, Jacob Whitmer, Peter Whitmer Jr., John Whitmer, and Hiram Page. Hiram was Peter Whitmer Sr.'s son-in-law. The other two men were from the Smith family: Joseph Sr. and Hyrum.[7] According to Lucy, the eight men "repaired to a little grove where it was customary for the family to offer up their secret prayers," and "those eight witnesses . . . looked upon the plates and handled them."[8]

Based on the statement that these eight witnesses attested to regarding the gold plates, Samuel must have been thrilled to see and handle the plates. Samuel no longer needed to have faith in the existence of the plates. His belief was now based on what he personally had seen. And he knew he was part of a rather exclusive group. With this knowledge, Samuel's devotion to his brother Joseph would have only deepened.

Some writers have subsequently claimed that Samuel either lied about seeing the plates or was deceived by his brother Joseph into thinking he saw gold plates. However, the historical record suggests that Samuel seemed sincere in his claims about seeing the plates. A trait often associated with Samuel is integrity. His straightforward expressions in his journal appear honest and genuine. Samuel's neighbors described him as friendly, good-natured, and respected. His family and close associates consistently portrayed Samuel as unassuming, reliable, and sincere. The idea that he would intentionally deceive on a large scale seems inconsistent with Samuel's overall character, based on how his contemporaries described him. (Samuel's positive reputation sharply contrasts with that of his brother William.) Furthermore, Samuel was not afraid to question his older siblings, including Joseph, when necessary; he had not been "easily persuaded" by what Joseph told him about a month earlier. Samuel does not seem to have believed that his brother Joseph deceived him.

In the fall of 1829, Joseph arranged for Egbert B. Grandin, a printer from Palmyra, to print the translation of the plates. The title of the translated manuscript was the Book of Mormon. Martin Harris sold part of his farm for $3,000.00 to finance the printing of the book. In March 1830, the Book of Mormon was published.[9] The statements from Cowdery, Harris, David Whitmer, and the other eight men who claimed to have seen the plates were printed along with the Book of Mormon and are included in copies of the book to this day. Joseph and the entire Smith family must have been relieved.

CHAPTER 16

No Turning Back

Sometime in March 1830, representatives of the Western Presbyterian Church in Palmyra visited Lucy, Hyrum, and Samuel. One of the representatives, Deacon Beckwith, tried to persuade the Smiths not to neglect their worship at the church or speak about the plates that Joseph had found. Lucy, Hyrum, and Samuel refused.

Samuel boldly quoted a passage of scripture from Isaiah to the deacon: "His watchmen are blind: they are all ignorant, they are dumb dogs, they cannot bark; sleeping, lying down, loving to slumber. Yea, they are greedy dogs which can never have enough, and they are shepherds that cannot understand; they all look to their own way, every one for his gain, from his quarter" (Isaiah 56:10–11).

Upon hearing Samuel's words, the representatives quickly departed. Addressing a church official in such a manner was quite bold. Apparently, Samuel wanted to make a statement to show his conviction about his brother's work. Having studied the Bible with his family over the years, Samuel was familiar with biblical texts and, to some extent, had a working knowledge of the scriptures, as shown by his interaction with Deacon Beckwith. Records from the Western Presbyterian Church documented that the Smiths "acknowledged that they had

43

entirely neglected the ordinances of the church for the last eighteen months and that they did not wish to unite with us any more." They were therefore "suspended."[1]

The Smiths had always struggled to stay united in their religious beliefs. By early 1830, they had completely separated their spiritual life from any existing Christian denomination or movement, as evidenced by their exclusion from the Presbyterian church of Palmyra.

During this period in early nineteenth-century America, the country promoted the ideal of the "common man," and Americans frequently rejected social and political elitism in favor of a more egalitarian and democratic society.[2] However, the idea of egalitarianism at that time was limited, as it only applied to white males. To support these ideas, throughout the 1820s and 1830s, various states began expanding voting rights to all white males over twenty-one by removing property requirements and other restrictions.[3] The expanding frontier also created opportunities and seemed to offer control over one's destiny. Individual progress and the desire for certainty were underlying motivations for many Americans.

Perhaps the impulses and ideals embedded in early America influenced and fostered confidence within the Smith family as they embraced their distinctive and new religious path in a united manner. Samuel, being a strong and serious-minded young man, must have been motivated to confidently embark on and navigate his life while remaining loyal to his family and the religious movement founded by his brother. The Smith family was united in their religious beliefs for the first time.

CHAPTER 17

The Six and the First

On April 6, 1830, the day designated to officially establish the new church, about forty people gathered at the log home of Peter and Mary Whitmer in Fayette to witness the event. As required by New York law, six charter members were chosen to form the new church. The church's name on the day it was organized was the Church of Christ. The six charter members were Joseph Jr., Hyrum, Oliver Cowdery, Peter Whitmer Jr., David Whitmer, and Samuel.

Soon after, Samuel was rebaptized as a member of the new church, presumably in Seneca Lake or Kendig Creek, near the Whitmer farm. Others were baptized as well. Samuel was also ordained to the Aaronic Priesthood. Within a few months, all of Samuel's immediate family members were baptized. On April 11, the first public church service was held at the Whitmer home.[1]

Shortly after the Church of Christ was officially organized, Samuel returned to Manchester. There, Joseph said, he received a revelation, directed to Samuel, that Samuel was "under no condemnation" and that his calling "is to exhortation, and to strengthen the church."[2] The revelation made clear that Samuel was "not as yet called to preach before the world." Samuel must have been expecting a call to preach, but the revelation given to him did imply that he would be called as a missionary at some point in the future.

Samuel joined family members in Fayette in early June to attend the first conference of the Church of Christ. At the conference, Joseph ordained Samuel to the Melchizedek Priesthood and as an elder in the church. Within a few weeks, Joseph also called Samuel to serve as a missionary for the church in the surrounding areas of Palmyra.[3] This was the first time Joseph had officially called anyone to serve as a missionary for the church.

Samuel must have been excited about the prospect of being called the first missionary of the nascent church. Yet with that excitement came some apprehension. Samuel had no training in religion or proselytizing, and there was no template or instruction book for him to follow. Furthermore, Samuel was not known to be a particularly articulate speaker or eloquent orator. Regardless of such concerns, he certainly was not fearful. Yet Samuel would experience disappointment on this mission because of the negative response he received from most of those he encountered, and he didn't baptize anyone. His mission would prove to be emotionally draining and physically taxing.

Ultimately, though, time would show that Samuel achieved long-lasting success in impacting the future of the newly founded faith through his efforts on this mission. His missionary activities helped propel a small, local religious movement into a vibrant, national religion that would polarize a still young nation.

CHAPTER 18

Samuel and the Seeds of the Future

Samuel left on his first missionary journey on June 30, 1830, travelling by foot. According to his mother, Samuel traveled about twenty-five miles on the first day of his mission. Along the way, he stopped at several places to talk about and sell copies of the Book of Mormon "but was turned out of doors" each time. As evening approached, he had one last encounter at an inn. The landlord called Samuel a "liar." Samuel was "sick at heart." He quickly left and found a small brook. At the brook, he "washed his feet" as a "testimony against the man."[1]

The ritual of washing feet in this context seems to have originated in the New Testament. In Matthew 10:14, Jesus commands his disciples to preach and adds: "and whosoever shall not receive you, nor hear your words, when ye depart out of that house or city, shake off the dust of your feet." There is a similar command in the Gospel of Luke. Perhaps as a continuation of this practice, Joseph claimed a revelation in July 1830 that advised: "And in whatsoever place ye shall enter, and they receive you not in my name, ye shall leave a cursing instead of a blessing, by casting the dust of your feet against them as a testimony and cleansing your feet by the wayside."[2]

Joseph surely discussed this idea with Samuel, and perhaps some others, before this revelation and before Samuel left on his first mission on the last day of June. Samuel felt strongly about employing the ritual, as he had been hungry when he was rejected; not only did the landlord reject his message, but he also didn't offer him any sustenance.

Samuel walked several miles further and slept under an "apple tree a short distance from the road." The ground was "cold" and "damp." In the morning, Samuel found a small cottage where he was offered some food.[3] After walking several more miles, Samuel left a copy of the Book of Mormon at John P. Greene's house in Mendon, New York. Mr. Greene was a Methodist preacher and didn't seem very interested in the book Samuel gave him.

Later, Samuel returned to the Greene home and spoke with Mrs. Rhoda Young Greene. She told him she had read the book and was "much pleased with it." Samuel told her she could keep the book. As he was about to leave, Mrs. Greene asked Samuel to pray with her. Decades later, Lucy Mack Smith recalled what Rhoda Greene had related to her about Samuel—that, when they prayed that day, Mrs. Greene "never saw a man that had such an appearance or ever heard such a prayer in her life." "My God," she said, "it seemed as though the very heavens were rent and the Spirit of God was poured down upon us." Mrs. Greene later persuaded her husband to read the Book of Mormon, and he also became converted to its message. Months later, they were both baptized into the new church. Mrs. Greene shared the book and her testimony about it with her family as well.[4]

Around this time, Samuel also met Phineas Young, a Methodist preacher and brother of Rhoda Young Greene, at the Tomlinson Inn in Mendon, New York. As Phineas later recalled, a young man came in, and walking across the room to where I was sitting, held a book toward me, saying — "There is a book, sir, I wish you to read."

The thing appeared so novel to me that for a moment I hesitated, saying — "Pray sir, what book have you?"

"The Book of Mormon, or, as it is called by some, the Golden Bible."

"Ah, sir, then it purports to be a revelation."

"Yes," said he, "it is a revelation from God."

I took the book, and by his request looked at the testimony of the witnesses. Said he — "If you will read this book with a prayerful heart, and ask God to give you a witness, you will know the truth of this work."

I told him I would do so, and then asked him his name. He said his name was Samuel H. Smith. "Ah," said I, "you are one of the witnesses."

"Yes," said he, "I know the book to be a revelation from God, translated by the gift and power of the Holy Ghost, and that my brother, Joseph Smith, Jun., is a prophet, seer and revelator."[5]

Phineas soon read the Book of Mormon and believed it was true. Rhoda and Phineas's brother, Brigham Young, also read one of their copies of the Book of Mormon and was impressed. Brigham then shared his thoughts on the Book of Mormon with his neighbor and friend, Heber C. Kimball. After further investigation, both Heber and Brigham were baptized, along with the rest of the Young family.

Although Samuel seemed to have little immediate success on this mission, his efforts in distributing the Book of Mormon were directly responsible for the conversion of consequential future church leaders. Without Samuel's proselytizing efforts, the Young family and Kimball might never have connected with the church. As such, Samuel significantly altered the course of the history of The Church of Jesus Christ of Latter-day Saints. Brigham Young later served as the President of the Church, succeeding Joseph Smith Jr., and led tens of thousands of members nearly 1,300 miles from Nauvoo, Illinois, to Salt Lake City beginning in 1846. Heber C. Kimball and Phineas Young also held prominent roles within the church.

CHAPTER 19

Family and Church Matters

A second church conference was scheduled in late September in Fayette. Samuel attended the three-day event. Joseph Jr., the First Elder of the Church of Christ, addressed purported revelations that church member Hiram Page said he had received through a stone. After some discussion, the conference, along with Hiram Page, agreed to renounce the revelations and established that only Joseph Smith Jr. was appointed to receive and write revelations and commandments for the church. This development likely pleased Samuel, as he had faith in his brother's revelatory communications and could not imagine anyone else in that role. The minutes of this conference also recorded that the small but growing church had sixty-two members at that time.[1]

About a month later, Samuel's father was taken to a debtors' prison in Canandaigua for failing to pay a fourteen-dollar debt. Canandaigua, a village fourteen miles south of Palmyra, served as the seat of Ontario County, New York, and had a relatively large population of about 5,200 at that time.[2]

After a couple of days, Samuel returned home fatigued from his missionary journey. He had "taken a heavy cold, and [his] bones ache[d] dreadfully." His mother explained what had happened to his father. The next morning at sunrise, Samuel left for Canandaigua, where he was allowed to see his father. He was concerned about his father and the conditions of his imprisonment. Samuel tenderly brought some "comfortable food" for his father and spent the night with him. Soon after, Joseph Sr. started working at a cooper's shop in the jail yard, and he earned enough money to pay his debt after about thirty days. Samuel, having finished his mission, returned to his log home in Palmyra around the same time his father was released from the Canandaigua jail.[3]

Later that fall, at Joseph Jr.'s direction, the Smith family moved from Palmyra to a home near Waterloo, New York. Some in the Waterloo area stated that Joseph had taken on work there before the Smith family arrived. Waterloo was also just a few miles from Fayette. Since Joseph was familiar with the area and it was close to Fayette, he likely considered it a good place to relocate his family. It appears that the Smiths moved into a house owned by Fuller Kellog. The house was situated on the Seneca River in an area called "The Kingdom," located between Waterloo and Seneca Falls. Samuel was instrumental in the move.

According to Lucy, shortly after arriving in The Kingdom,

We were made to realize that the hearts of the people were in the hands of the Lord; for we had scarcely unpacked our goods, when one of our new neighbors, a Mr. Osgood, came in and invited us to drive our stock and teams to his barnyard, and feed them from his barn, free of cost, until we could make further arrangements. Many of our neighbors came and welcomed us. . . . Among whom was Mr. Hooper, a tavern keeper, whose wife came with him, and brought us a present of some delicate eatables. Such manifestations of kindness as these were shown us from day to day, during our continuance in the place. And they were duly appreciated, for we had experienced the opposite so severly, that the least show of good feeling gave rise to the liveliest sensations of gratitude.

As Lucy also reported during their residence there, "We established the practice of spending the evenings in singing and praying. The neighbors soon became aware of this, and it caused our house to become a place of evening resort for some dozen or twenty persons."[4]

Leaving the small confines of their log home was certainly bittersweet. They had many fond memories of living in the Palmyra/Manchester area for nearly fifteen years, and countless momentous events had occurred there. Yet they also had faced tragedy, hostility, and difficulties. As the Smith family adopted their new religious paradigm, some former neighbors in Palmyra became critical of them. With the publicity surrounding the "Gold Bible" and Joseph's new religious movement, several former neighbors claimed the Smith family was "poorly educated," "ignorant," and "selfish." It seems most such criticisms appeared after the Book of Mormon was published and Joseph's role as a prophet became known.

At least one neighbor claimed that "every one [of them] drank." This likely was the case. The early nineteenth century saw widespread alcohol consumption, even among young people; there was no defined "drinking age" in early America. However, there is no strong historical evidence to suggest that the Smiths drank more alcohol than was typical during that time. Perhaps the harshest critic of Joseph Sr.'s drinking was Joseph Sr. himself. Temperance movements in the United

States did not begin in earnest until the 1830s. Joseph Jr. did claim a revelation discouraging alcohol consumption a few years later, in 1833. This revelation became known as the Word of Wisdom. Even then, as suggested by this appellation, the revelation was essentially considered wise advice, not a commandment from God. Despite the accusations of drinking, even some critics of the Smiths acknowledged that the Smith boys did "a good day[']s work."[5]

CHAPTER 20

Native Americans

In 1830, US President Andrew Jackson signed the Indian Removal Act, which authorized the president to negotiate the relocation of Native Americans to lands west of the Mississippi River. This legislation led to the forced removal of the Cherokee people from their ancestral lands in Georgia, Tennessee, Alabama, and North Carolina during 1838–39. This tragic event, known as the Trail of Tears, led to the deaths of thousands of Native American men, women, and children. Other tribes were forced to relocate as well.[1]

Ironically, just a few months after Congress passed the Indian Removal Act, Joseph Smith called missionaries to preach the gospel to the "Lamanites" (a group of people described in the Book of Mormon and considered to be among the ancestors of Native Americans). This call came about three months after Samuel received his call as the first Latter-day Saint missionary.[2] Although Samuel was not specifically assigned to proselytize Native Americans, he met noted Native American preacher William Apess in Boston while on a mission with Orson Hyde a few years later.

Samuel recorded his encounter with Apess: "Visited by a man by the name of Apes[s] an Indian of the Peyrd [Pequod] tribe he was a Preacher though some unbelieveing at first but

55

became more belileveing & concluded to give the work a candid investigation & invited us to Preach in his hall [Franklin Hall] that hireed to preach in himself & also invited us to pay him a visit we concluded to go to Prividence & we told him that we would when we returned."[3]

The encounter appeared respectful and positive. According to one scholar, what Samuel and Hyde "almost certainly did not realize was that the 'Indian Missionary' with whom they conversed was on his way to becoming one of the foremost Native American evangelists and activists in antebellum America." Apess published the first Native American autobiography in America, among other notable works.[4]

CHAPTER 21

The Ohio

"Ye shall go to the Ohio," Joseph Jr. wrote as divine instruction in January 1831. A few months earlier, Oliver Cowdery and others had been called by Joseph to proselytize in Ohio. Many of the converts from their missionary efforts lived near the town of Kirtland, Ohio. As such, a small congregation (referred to as a branch) was soon established there. At the third church conference in Fayette in January 1831, Joseph announced that the church was to gather in Ohio; Kirtland was designated as the specific gathering place. Accordingly, Kirtland became the church's headquarters. It was not long before more than half of Kirtland's population were members of the church.[1]

During this period, Joseph called Samuel to serve a second mission, this time around Kirtland, along with recent convert Orson Pratt. Samuel's dedication to his brother and his church work seemed to be his main focus. But the fruits of his missionary efforts would eventually alter his circumstances. Soon after, Katharine Smith married Wilkins Salisbury in Kirtland.[2] With Katharine married, Samuel and William remained the only Smith siblings of marriageable age who had not yet married.

Joseph and Emma moved to Kirtland in February 1831.[3] Joseph Sr., Lucy, Samuel, and the rest of the family soon followed. Since the church had not yet built meetinghouses in Kirtland, members met either outside or in someone's home. Later, meetings were held in the Kirtland schoolhouse.[4] Newspapers in New York and Pennsylvania highlighted that a Black man named Peter, presumably a convert, was worshipping with church members in Kirtland.[5]

Samuel served with Pratt on the Ohio mission until April 1831. During this mission, Samuel and Pratt baptized about fifty people. Many of the converts had previously been part of the faith community led by Alexander Campbell.[6] This community had roots in the Restorationist movement. The goal of that movement was to restore the lost beliefs and practices of Jesus to the Christian community. As a result, many of the concepts taught by Samuel and Pratt resonated with this community. Samuel and Pratt were elated by their success.

When his mission ended, Samuel, along with his mother, father, and siblings, briefly stayed at Isaac Morley's farm in northern Kirtland. Morley had been baptized into the church just a few months earlier. Joseph and Emma were among those staying at the Morley farm.

While there, Emma gave birth to twins, Thaddeus and Louisa. Tragically, the twins only lived about three hours after birth. Around the same time, church member Julia Murdock in Kirtland also gave birth to twins. While her husband John was excited about the birth of their twins, he was devastated when his wife, Julia, died soon afterward. John Murdock, who already had three young children, urged Joseph and Emma to adopt his twin babies. The Murdock twins, Joseph Murdock Smith and Julia Smith, were quickly adopted and warmly welcomed by Joseph and Emma, along with the rest of the Smith family.[7]

CHAPTER 22

More Missions

The next general conference of the church was held in June 1831 in Kirtland. Samuel was ordained a high priest at this conference. Along with many others, Samuel was called to serve another mission. He was assigned to serve in Missouri with Reynolds Cahoon.[1] Samuel and Cahoon left soon after and "preached the gospel without purse or script, enduring much for want of food and rest."

Along with other missionaries, Samuel and Cahoon traveled through Indiana and Illinois, albeit on different routes, on their way to Independence, Missouri. As they traveled through Illinois, several church branches were established in the state. In Paris, Illinois, Samuel and Cahoon met William McLellin, a store clerk, and they asked if "they had any preaching evenings in the place." McLellin responded, "Yes," and quickly organized a large gathering in "a convenient room." After Samuel and Cahoon preached, McLellin asked them to stay and preach again. They replied that they had to continue their journey to Independence. The evening after they left, McLellin was "unable to sleep." Eventually, he traveled on horseback to Independence, where he was soon baptized. While passing through western Illinois, Samuel and Cahoon briefly stopped in the small town of Quincy. They preached the church's first sermon there.[2] The next time Samuel returned to Quincy, it would be under dire circumstances.

By early August, Samuel and Cahoon arrived in Independence. At that time, Independence was a small frontier village far less developed than Kirtland. A few weeks earlier, Joseph Jr. had arrived in Independence and proclaimed it the "center place" and the future "city of Zion." By mid-August, Samuel and Cahoon started their journey back to Kirtland, reassured by Joseph's statement that God was "well pleased" with them.[3] Meanwhile, the first signs of trouble began to surface within the frontier community. Samuel and Cahoon returned to Kirtland in late September. Unbeknownst to Samuel, equally serious problems awaited at Kirtland in the near future.

The next church conference was held in early October 1831 in Orange Township, just a few miles south of Kirtland. Samuel attended the conference, where he was called to serve another mission in eastern Ohio. His new missionary companion was William McLellin, whom Samuel had been instrumental in converting to the church just a few months earlier during his last mission.[4] Before they left, a revelation given to McLellin from Joseph warned him to "Forsake all unrighteousness. Commit not adultery- a temptation with which thou has been troubled."[5] Early in their mission, McLellin recorded in his journal that Samuel laid his hands on a child who had been burned, and the child was healed "in so much that it did not even so much as blister." Lucy later said that none of her sons had a greater gift of healing than Samuel.

Despite witnessing this healing, McLellin faced personal struggles and returned to Kirtland in late December. Joseph later said that McLellin had "murmurings [in his] heart."

Samuel recorded in his journal that "because of disobedience, our Way was hedged up before us. Brother William was taken sick." McLellin recorded in his journal that "my cold increased and my breast and lungs became so exceeding sore I was cast down upon my bed and mostly confined." As a result, Samuel and McLellin's mission lasted only about forty days.[6]

CHAPTER 23

The Long, Life-Changing Mission

At the January 1832 conference held in Amherst, Ohio, Samuel was called to missionary service once again. Joseph instructed him to serve with Orson Hyde in the New England area. Samuel and Hyde embarked on their mission in early February 1832.[1] Traveling mainly on foot and occasionally by stagecoach, they covered two thousand miles. During their journey, they stopped to preach in schoolhouses, taverns, stores, churches, and private homes, sharing their message in many cities and towns across Ohio, New York, Pennsylvania, Connecticut, Rhode Island, Massachusetts, Vermont, and Maine.

The "toilsome" missionary journey took a physical toll on Samuel and Hyde at times. One time, Hyde's "feet were lame, being blistered," and Samuel at one point had "taken sick with a chill fever." To sustain their journey, they "got [their] boots mended" and had extra clothes made for them.[2] While some who listened to their preaching were receptive, most were not. Nevertheless, they baptized about sixty people and established four branches of the church on this nearly year-long mission. Samuel and Hyde organized one branch in Maine, two in Massachusetts, and one in Pennsylvania.[3]

A few months earlier, Joseph Jr. and Emma had moved to Hiram, Ohio, to live at the John Johnson farm. It was here that Joseph continued working on a revised version of the Bible that he had started as early as June 1830. The revision, which came to be known as the Inspired Version or the Joseph Smith Translation, was intended to clarify the meaning of various passages and restore ideas/context that had been lost from the original writings of the biblical authors. Using the text of the King James Version, Joseph clarified and expanded various scripture passages throughout the Bible. The revision was not meant as a literal textual translation of the original writings.

In March 1832, while Samuel was traveling on his mission with Hyde, a mob broke into the Johnson farmhouse during the early morning and carried Joseph and church leader Sidney Rigdon outside. Joseph was already outside before he was completely awake. The mob tore Joseph's and Sidney's clothes and proceeded to hit and kick them. In the process, one of Joseph's teeth was knocked out. Joseph struggled, kicking a member of the mob in the face. The man subsequently grabbed Joseph by the throat and choked him until he was unconscious. A bucket of hot tar and feathers was then smeared over Joseph and Sidney's bodies. After the mob left, Joseph slowly regained consciousness and struggled back to the farmhouse. When Emma saw his battered body, she fainted. Friends spent the night peeling and scraping tar off their bodies, sometimes taking off layers of skin with it.[4] Such violence was certainly sobering for Joseph and his family. When Samuel heard of the violence against his brother, he must have been emotional, angry, and wary.

In early 1832, in Springfield, Massachusetts, as Samuel and Hyde traveled eastward on their missionary journey, they met Daniel Tyler. Daniel seemed to be impressed with the missionary message Samuel shared with him. Years later,

Daniel recorded that he had heard Samuel Smith speak that year about the "circumstances of the coming forth of the Book of Mormon, of which he said he was a witness. He knew his brother Joseph had the plates, for the prophet had shown them to him, and Samuel had handled them and seen the engravings thereon. His speech was more like a narrative than a sermon."[5] From Samuel's perspective, since he had firsthand knowledge of the plates and the translation of the Book of Mormon, it was natural for him to share his personal story rather than deliver a theologized oration. Daniel Tyler was later baptized and served in a prominent role in the church.

While in Oxford, Massachusetts, Samuel and Hyde visited Asael Hyde, Orson's brother. Asael was Methodist and, as Samuel described him, "hard and unbelieving" when they discussed the Book of Mormon and the church with him. Just before leaving Oxford, "Orson talked to him [Asael] for his unbelief, and he told him that he should see him no more and his heart was touched and it melted down into tears." Hyde was firm in his belief in the Book of Mormon, Joseph's prophethood, and the church, as was Samuel. Even family bonds were not as strong as Hyde's faith. Samuel records in his journal that they "bid him [Asael] adieu."[6]

Hyde had a tendency to sermonize at times. At a "Methodist Meeting House" with a "large congregation," Samuel recorded, "Brother Orson spoke unto them about two hours and then I spoke a short time." As this specific incident and several other entries in Samuel's missionary journal show, Samuel didn't demand a dominant role with his missionary companions. Samuel may have felt inadequate in many respects. Hyde recorded in his missionary journal that Samuel was "slow of speech and uneducated, yet a man of good faith and extreme integrity."[7] Consequently, Samuel might have felt more comfortable taking a "junior" role with Hyde as his missionary companion. Others mentioned that Samuel was not as eloquent as his older brothers or his missionary companions.[8] Nevertheless, Samuel was genuinely sincere and expressed his feelings honestly.

Undoubtedly, Samuel's attributes helped him deliver an effective spiritual message. Later, Samuel was considered "one of the foremost builders in the early years of the Church."[9] Samuel did not question his missionary role within the church founded by his brother Joseph. Still, other important roles for Samuel within the church were forthcoming.

Samuel and Hyde's faith in their mission was strong, and they sought divine guidance as they traveled. At one point, Samuel recorded that they "calculated to go to New Haven, but the Lord directed us different. Pressed to and went on our way to Boston." During their time in Boston, Samuel and Hyde faced some confrontational "priests" who "began to come and see us, and they would strive to catch us in our words."[10] Despite this, Samuel and Hyde successfully converted several people in Boston, including a man named Joseph T. Ball. A Boston resident of Black African descent, Ball soon moved to Kirtland and, after a few years, was ordained an elder. Later, Samuel's brother William ordained Ball to the office of high priest and installed him as Boston branch president in 1844.[11]

While in Boston, Samuel and Hyde also met Mary Bailey and Agnes Coolbrith. Both women were educated and refined. Mary attended the "famous Old South Church and sang in the church choir." After listening to Samuel and Hyde, Mary and Agnes were converted to their message. They were baptized in late June. Samuel baptized Mary.[12] Mary's twin sister and family "were greatly shocked when they learned what [she] had done, and – much to [her] disappointment- they would not listen to her. . . . she was forced to make a choice between [her family] and her new religion!"[13] It was difficult for Mary to be disowned by her family. But her newfound convictions ran deep. She was supported by friends who had recently been baptized. One such friend was Augusta Cobb.

After Samuel and Hyde left, Augusta told Mary, "dear, some day you will go to Kirtland, and become the wife of Samuel Smith." Mary blushed and asked, "Oh sister Cobb, do you really think so?"[14] Apparently, Augusta sensed a natural attraction between Samuel and Mary. Samuel's granddaughter later wrote that Samuel and Mary had a "love which had been unconsciously kindled in Boston."[15]

While still in Boston, Samuel and Hyde were expounding on their beliefs at a meeting, and as Samuel explained, they were

> somewhat interrupted this day in the meeting by a man and woman that taught the doctrine of the devil, such as abstaining from meat and having spiritual wives and so forth. They came to our meeting. The woman arose and began to preach and we requested her to stop and she would not, and we cried against her spirit, for we knew that it was an unclean spirit, and we cried against it that it was of the devil, and it made considerable stir. The man that had the same spirit tempted us, saying: "Cast the Devil out," crying amen to the words of the woman. After considerable muttering and grumbling and shaking of her frame, she stopped and we proceeded with our meeting.[16]

Based on his description of this rather unsettling situation, the outbursts by this man and woman didn't appear to disturb Samuel in any significant way.

As Samuel and Hyde continued their missionary journey, they encountered various situations that prompted them to heal, pray, or rebuke. On one occasion, Samuel recorded that they "laid hands on a sister that had been sick with the ague [fever and chills often associated with malaria] for some time and she was filled with the Spirit of the Lord and she thought the disease was removed."[17] Samuel wrote in his missionary journal that, while eating breakfast, "there was a man in bondage of the Devil and he said he could not get repentance nor faith. He took us into a room by himself and told us his situation and took us by the hands and kissed our hands and required us to pray for him, but he did not obtain relief; he could exercise no faith and he was truly a distressed object. He said that he had enjoyed the Grace of God in days past."[18] Samuel seemed to be sympathetic toward this man but ultimately could not secure a positive outcome regarding his mental and emotional state or convert him to the church.

While in Providence, Rhode Island, Samuel and Hyde were "threatened with tar and feathering."[19] Although the threat never materialized, it must have been terrifying for them. At Fox Point, just outside Providence, Samuel and Hyde met Vienna Jaques during the summer of 1832. Vienna lived in Boston but also had a home near Providence. She had traveled to Kirtland and was baptized in the church the previous summer. As a woman of considerable financial means, she worked as a nurse and midwife. Samuel and Hyde stayed with her in Providence and later in Boston.

Vienna's sister Harriet was married to James Angel; they had a son together. James was hostile toward Samuel and Hyde. He warned Samuel and Hyde that Harriet was not to be baptized. Vienna confided in Samuel and Hyde that Mr. Angel only married her sister for money and that he was abusive to her. She worried that her sister's life might be in danger. Harriet wanted to be baptized and move to Independence, Missouri. James must have become aware of or strongly suspected Harriet's feelings, as he confronted Samuel and Hyde, saying they had "sowed the seeds of discord in [my] family." Samuel recorded in his journal that James surmised that we "persuad[ed] his woman to leave him." Samuel and Hyde advised Vienna to help Harriet according to her wishes, but only after they had left the area. As such, Samuel and Hyde quickly left in the early hours of the morning.[20]

While in York County, Maine, Samuel and Hyde met with members of the Society of Free Brethren movement. Also known as the Cochranites, the Society of Free Brethren was founded by Jacob Cochran (sometimes spelled "Cochrane"), a charismatic orator who initially was affiliated with the Freewill Baptist movement. Notably, the Cochranite movement became known for practicing frenzied dancing, communal living, and the rejection of marriage vows in favor of polygamous relationships they called "spiritual wifery." Samuel recorded in his journal that they "went to a meeting in the evening and the people were called Cockrinites [*sic*] because the man that first preached their faith his name was Cockrin. They gave liberty for anyone to speak." After Hyde preached to them, Samuel said that "they would not let us preach [anymore] and there was a great confusion among them."

After preaching at another meeting in the same area, Samuel recalled, a "man arose and said that there had been a deceiver through that country and had deceived the people . . . and . . . if we had fellowship with that people that had been deceived (Kockranites [*sic*]) he should desire us to depart out of their coast. . . . We told him our mission was unto all people and we did not believe in the doctrine of the Kockranites." Regarding the same incident, Hyde recorded in his journal that he said that "our message was from God, and it was as much to Cochranites as Free Will Baptists, and that I should rejoice as much to see a Cochranite redeemed from his errors as a Free Will Baptist. But I told them I had no fellowship with error nor iniquity."

A few days afterward, Hyde recorded: "Visited three families but without much hope of doing anything to profit them because of the Cochranite's a deluded sect of people, by whom many had been deceived." A few days later, Hyde recorded: "preached to a congregation of Cochranites who gave liberty; told them to repent. . . . they had a wonderful lustful spirit, because they believe in a 'Plurality of wives' which they call spiritual wives, knowing them not after the flesh but after the spirit, but by the appearance they know one another after the flesh." It appears Hyde opined in his journal that the Cochranite men and women had been physically intimate with one another despite being called "spiritual" wives. It was clear that both Samuel and Hyde disapproved of the practices of the Society of Free Brethren, including the idea of "spiritual wifery."[21]

Decades later, starting in 1877, it was suggested that the practice and belief in polygamy within the Latter-day Saint faith originated from the Cochranite doctrine of "spiritual wifery." This claim points to Samuel and Hyde's contact with members of the Cochranite movement during their missionary journey in 1832, the first known interaction between church members and Cochranites.

While it may be tempting to draw a connection between the two phenomena, the historical evidence indicates otherwise. Significant evidence shows that Joseph Jr. discussed polygamous marriages as early as July 1831, well before Samuel began his mission to New England in 1832 and before any contact with those associated with the Society of Free Brethren movement.[22] There is no evidence that Samuel knew about Joseph's teaching of polygamy in 1831, as he was on a mission with Reynolds Cahoon traveling through Illinois at the time. Although Samuel's and Hyde's journals show that their feelings about the theology and ideas of the Society of Free Brethren were decidedly negative, the two later accepted seemingly similar ideas within the religious movement they embraced.

In the early nineteenth century, America underwent significant economic, social, and political changes that fostered reform movements, utopian ventures, and religious liberalism and experimentation. Unsurprisingly, ideas about love, courtship, sex, and marriage were reconsidered in light of the ideals of equality and democracy, coupled with socio-political reforms and religious movements that introduced new social paradigms. As a result, various social and religious movements and communities emerged during this period, including the Society of Free Brethren movement, the Oneida Community, New Harmony, Brook Farm, the Fruitlands community, Adventism, Dispensationalism, and the Shaker movement. These movements featured a wide range of responses to traditional views of love and marriage, such as relaxing patriarchal marriage customs, advocating for women's marital rights, and promoting celibacy, free love, and polygamous relationships.[23] It was perhaps inevitable that Samuel would encounter such ideas during his missionary work and within the new religious movement he and his family embraced.

Aside from his negative thoughts on polygamous relationships as recorded in his diary in 1832, there are no historical records indicating that Samuel opposed polygamy when his brother Joseph later introduced the practice to a small group of church members in Nauvoo. Since his brothers Joseph, Hyrum, and William practiced polygamy in the early 1840s, it seems unlikely that Samuel was unaware of the practice by then. There is no documented evidence suggesting that Samuel ever practiced polygamy, however. Perhaps Samuel had no interest in introducing polygamy to his wife. We can only speculate why Samuel was critical of polygamy as practiced by the Society of Free Brethren movement yet accepted it as a principle taught and practiced by Joseph. Hyrum initially struggled with the idea of polygamy.[24] Perhaps Joseph's explanation of polygamy within the theological context of eternal relationships, as taught by Joseph, helped Samuel accept his brother's teachings.

Samuel also struggled during this mission. In the late fall of 1832, he felt uncertain about his missionary efforts. Samuel believed he was "not faithful in prayer" and in "laboring in the vineyard attending to the things that the Lord had commanded [him]." His feelings of inadequacy persisted for at least a few weeks. Later, he wrote, "I should desire to return to Kirtland soon if I did not feel different in my mind, for I felt weak in my mind because of unfaithfulness. My faith had become weak in the Lord." Samuel made it clear he did not doubt the value of his work as a missionary, but he believed that he "had transgressed against the Lord" and "felt down in [his] mind." Hyde experienced similar feelings. During this time, Hyde recorded in his journal, "We felt cast down in our minds, and death in our hearts; and we went away into the woods by ourselves, and then we had a general time of confessing our faults, and we confessed everything we could think of, and then confessed them before the Lord; and we felt much better and our hearts were softened into tenderness." Samuel prayed for strength and admitted that he had been "backyard about taking the lead in meeting[s] and had Brother Orson take the lead" and "felt that [he] must be more faithful and stand in [his] lot."[25]

A few weeks later, Joseph Jr. sent a letter to Samuel and Hyde in Boston. The letter instructed them to return immediately to Kirtland. Samuel and Hyde arrived there in late December. Just before they arrived, Emma gave birth to Joseph Smith III at the Newel K. Whitney Store in Kirtland.[26]

CHAPTER 24

Kirtland and Independence

Joseph Jr. said that the Lord wanted a temple built in Kirtland, where Joseph hoped to organize what he called the "School of the Prophets." As a prerequisite for attending the school, elders had to participate in the ordinance of washing feet. At the school's first meeting in January 1833 in the upper room of the Whitney store, Samuel and other elders gathered as the "first laborers in his last vineyard." They prayed and fasted and "wash[ed] their hands and feet for a testimony that their garments [were] clean," prompting Samuel to record in his journal, "Thus my garments are clean from the blood of all men." Soon after, Samuel also recorded that he "attended the School some, but chief of the time, I've labored my hands," for the "Lord revealed that I should tarry at home."[1]

In February 1833, Samuel's younger brother William married Caroline A. Grant.[2] This left only Samuel, Don Carlos, and Lucy unmarried among the Smith siblings. During the summer of 1833, Mary Bailey moved from Boston to Kirtland. Samuel had baptized her during his mission to Boston the previous year. Mary's friend Agnes Coolbrith also moved with her to Kirtland. They both stayed with the Smith family upon their arrival. Mary and Agnes felt comfortable in their new surroundings. Along with Mary, Agnes had been disowned by her family when she was baptized into the new church. Mary and Agnes "soon learned to love Mother Smith's family as their own."[3] Samuel must have been happy with Mary's living arrangement. No doubt he showered Mary with attention and adulation. Whatever affinity they had for each other in Boston was easily nurtured in their new setting.

Meanwhile, plans for the Kirtland Temple advanced. In late July, Samuel participated in the cornerstone-laying ceremony. Construction on the temple started in earnest. Samuel deeply believed in the spiritual significance of the temple; he dedicated significant time and energy to helping build the temple over the next three years. Mary and Agnes spent most of their time making and mending clothes for the temple workers.[4]

That summer in Independence, William W. Phelps, editor of the church newspaper, the *Evening and Morning Star*, published an editorial titled "Free People of Color." The editorial caused a stir among residents of the slave state of Missouri who interpreted the editorial as encouraging free people of color to migrate to Independence. Within days, residents gathered and decided that the church had to be driven out of Independence and Jackson County. On July 20, a mob attacked and destroyed the church's printing press. Besides the *Evening and Morning Star* newspaper, the press was printing a collection of Joseph Smith's revelations called *A Book of Commandments*. The mob scattered the printed but unbound sheets of these revelations. Soon after, a few brave church members—Vienna Jaques, Mary Elizabeth Rollins, and her sister Caroline—gathered as many of the unbound sheets from the ground as they could.

It was later discovered that the last printed words on the unbound sheets read, "For verily I say that the rebellious are not of the blood of Ephraim." Those words later held deep spiritual meaning for many church members, reflecting their belief that the biblical tribe of Ephraim will gather Israel in the latter days. Ultimately, all church members in Jackson County were forced to move to neighboring counties in Missouri.[5]

Meanwhile, Joseph Jr. appointed Samuel to the Kirtland High Council in the newly formed Kirtland stake, which was the first stake organized in the church.[6] A stake is essentially one or several congregations within a geographic area and is roughly similar to a Catholic diocese. As a member of the high council in Kirtland, Samuel was a significant leader within the church. A few days after his appointment, Joseph Sr. blessed Samuel, saying that "[Samuel] shall be made a teacher in the house of the Lord, among the school of the prophets" and that the "Lord shall mature his mind and correct his judgment. . . . [Samuel] shall obtain the esteem and fellowship of his brethren . . . and also be an instrument in the hands of his God, in spreading abroad upon the mountains, and among all nations, the fulness of the everlasting gospel." In the blessing, Joseph also noted Samuel's "faithfulness and integrity of his soul."

The blessing illustrates how his father, and by extension, his family, viewed Samuel. He was regarded by his family and others as loyal and as having a significant impact on the church's proselytizing efforts. Later, Samuel was also appointed as an agent for the Literary Firm, which managed the church's publications.[7]

By February 1834, Joseph Smith Jr. stated that he received a revelation that Zion (Independence, Missouri) should be redeemed and that a group should be organized to travel there for that purpose. Joseph was troubled by what transpired in Independence following his declaration of it as the central gathering place and future city of Zion. By that summer, a group called the Camp of Israel, later referred to as Zion's Camp, had left Kirtland for Missouri. Approximately 230 individuals participated in the effort. Joseph, Hyrum, and William were all part of the camp. Samuel stayed in Kirtland. Within two months, Zion's Camp disbanded after failing to return church members to their lands and property in Independence.[8]

Perhaps unsurprisingly, Samuel and Mary started courting during this time. Their romantic feelings for each other continued. Samuel and Mary were married in August 1834, soon after Joseph, Hyrum, and William returned to Kirtland.[9]

CHAPTER 25

A Father's Blessing

In December 1833, Samuel's father was ordained as Church Patriarch. Days later, Joseph Sr. gathered his family for dinner and gave each of his children and their spouses a patriarchal blessing. Samuel's patriarchal blessing from his father stated that Samuel had "ministered comfort to thy father's family. . . . thou hast had a pure desire for the good of thy kindred." With these words, Joseph Sr. acknowledged Samuel's efforts and time in helping his parents and siblings, as well as his devotion to his family.

Joseph Sr. further said, "The just shall rise up and call thee, a perfect man. . . . Thou shalt be equal with thy brethren and thine inheritance shall be like unto theirs." Samuel was highly esteemed by his father. Joseph Sr. also recognized Samuel's missionary efforts by stating, "The testimony which thou has borne and shall bear, shall be received by thousands, and thou shalt magnify thy calling and do honor to the Holy Priesthood."

Joseph's blessing to Samuel's wife Mary must have been comforting to both her and Samuel. Joseph made it clear that Mary had become part of the Smith family: "Mary, my daughter-in-law, thou has been united to my family, and thy heart has believed the testimony of my son, and thou hast been faithful in keeping the commandments. Thou hast left thy father's house, and thy near relatives for the Gospel's sake. . . . For this thou art blessed. . . . thou dost greatly desire the spiritual good of thy kindred. . . . the Lord will hear thy prayers in their behalf, and they will yet come into the kingdom!"[1]

The love and unity Mary felt toward her in-laws is perhaps best illustrated in a letter she wrote to Joseph Jr.'s wife Emma during Christmas that year. In the letter, Mary described her family's Christmas as "some small gifts, not much but lots of love." She also expressed her love for Emma, telling her, "I love you, and we all do," and "I would give my life for you I know my family after me will do the same, you[r] family." Mary mentioned that her father-in-law told her and Samuel that they "would have a son and his son, of my son. Would be peacemakers to keeping good will in the family."[2] The closeness Mary felt toward the Smith family boded well for the newlywed couple.

CHAPTER 26

The First Child and a New Smith

The church's organizational structure continued to evolve. In February 1835, twelve persons were chosen to serve as special witnesses of Jesus Christ for the church. These Twelve Apostles would hold important leadership and administrative roles in the future. Joseph Smith, Oliver Cowdery, David Whitmer, and Martin Harris all participated in selecting the Twelve Apostles. Those chosen included Brigham Young, Heber C. Kimball, William McLellin, Orson Pratt, and William Smith. Eight of the twelve selected apostles had participated in Zion's Camp. William was among those chosen who had served as a member of Zion's Camp.

The selection process was not without some disagreements, however. Cowdery, Whitmer, and Harris initially chose Phineas Young to be one of the apostles. Joseph then requested that they select his brother William instead. According to Whitmer, Joseph wanted William to serve as an apostle because he believed "it was the only way which he [William] could be saved." Joseph had long been concerned about William's defiant and prideful nature. William himself seemed to confirm some of Joseph's concerns. He later described himself as "naturally high-spirited" and recalled that in his youth he was "quite wild and inconsiderate, paying no attention to religion of any kind, for which I received frequent lectures from my mother and my brother Joseph."[1] William had been a member of Zion's Camp, but it appears Joseph's concern for William's spiritual well-being was the reason he requested William serve as an apostle. In supporting his brother William, perhaps Joseph felt he couldn't comfortably advocate for his other brother Samuel to serve in the same role.

In late summer of 1835, the youngest Smith brother, Don Carlos, married Mary Bailey's friend Agnes Coolbrith.[2] Thus, Samuel's and Don Carlos's families became especially close. Within a few years, both families would be living on a farm together at a time when Mary and Agnes would need each other the most.

In August, Joseph's revelations, intended to be published two years earlier at Independence under the title *A Book of Commandments*, were finally published in Kirtland, along with additional revelations and seven essays (later known as *Lectures on Faith*). They were published under the title Doctrine and Covenants, which was soon accepted as scripture at a church conference (alongside the Bible and the Book of Mormon).[3] Samuel is mentioned seven times in the Doctrine and Covenants; most of these references relate to calls for missionary service.

During that summer, Joseph Jr. and others purchased four Egyptian mummies and several papyrus scrolls from antiques dealer Michael Chandler, who was visiting the Kirtland area. Joseph soon spent time "translating" the papyrus scrolls. Samuel was in Kirtland at the time of the purchase of the scrolls and during Joseph's initial efforts to translate them. Samuel likely saw and handled the Egyptian artifacts. However, Joseph was unable to complete the translation until 1842. Ultimately, the translated scrolls resulted in the Book of Abraham, which was later canonized when, in 1880, it was included in the Pearl of Great Price, the final book of church scripture. Samuel is mentioned twice in the Pearl of Great Price.[4]

In Ohio, as in many states during that time, all white adult males were required to serve in the state militia. Clergymen were exempt from this duty. In October, Samuel was charged with neglecting his military duties by failing to attend company and regimental musters in 1833. As such, Samuel was required to appear in court in Chardon, Ohio, about ten miles from Kirtland. Joseph Jr., Hyrum, and Don Carlos accompanied him to court. Samuel argued that he was exempt from military service because he was a clergyman. He was ordered to pay a twenty-dollar fine for not having the proper documents to prove his exemption. Short on money, Samuel sold one of his cows to pay the fine.[5] When Samuel returned to Kirtland, his wife Mary was very ill, pregnant, and about to give birth to their first child.

Mary's labor and delivery faced complications. Joseph Jr. recorded in his journal that she was in a "verry dangerous situation." As a result, Don Carlos quickly traveled to Chardon to seek help from church member and physician Frederick Williams. Joseph was so worried about Mary and her unborn child that he "went out into the field and bowed before the Lord and called upon him in mighty prayer." To everyone's relief, Mary gave birth to Susanna Bailey Smith, and both survived. Surprisingly, Mary's parents visited her during this time. It is the only known time they visited Mary after her conversion to the church and her move to Kirtland.[6] After the strife over her converting to the church, it must have been heartwarming for Mary that her parents visited during this period and saw their new granddaughter.

Despite Mary's estrangement from her birth family, she loved Samuel. In an undated letter, she declared that Samuel is "the best father and husband on earth" and referred to him as "[her] loving husband." It's equally clear that Samuel sincerely loved Mary. Mary also conveyed in the letter Samuel's strong allegiance to his family, stating that Samuel "shell live to take care of all you[r] bro Joseph and Hyrum needs."[7] In a tragic context, these words proved to be hauntingly accurate.

CHAPTER 27

Samuel and the Physical Altercation

Meanwhile, over the previous two months, tensions between Joseph and William had surfaced as they disagreed on several church-related issues. The conflict also affected Samuel.

Days after Susanna's birth, Joseph Jr. recorded in his diary that Samuel's mind was darkened. Joseph claimed that their brother William influenced Samuel's feelings. Uncharacteristically, Samuel was so upset that, as Joseph recalled, Samuel was "exclaiming" against Joseph in the streets of Kirtland. Joseph agonized over this conflict, praying that Samuel and William would receive "humility and repentance . . . [and for] heavenly Father to open their eyes . . . that they may extricate themselves from the snare they have fallen into." Samuel's feelings against his brother soon passed. Samuel was not one to hold a grudge.

William, often described as volatile and abrasive, was not easily dissuaded. In December, he instigated a physical confrontation with Joseph as a result of their months-long dispute. The altercation left Joseph "bruised and wounded . . . [and unable to] sit down or rise up without help" for some time. It was later said that Joseph occasionally felt the effects of the altercation until his death. Two days later, William apologized to Joseph in a letter.[1]

CHAPTER 28

A Spiritual and Physical Endowment

In November 1835, Joseph stated that priesthood holders "need an endowment . . . in order that you may be prepared and able to overcome all things." In early 1836, the Kirtland Temple was completed. Joseph held meetings with priesthood holders in the upper room of the temple. There, Joseph conducted ordinances that marked the beginning of what was later called the endowment ordinance. The dedication of the temple was held in late March. Nearly one thousand people attended the dedicatory services. Many later recorded that they experienced spiritual manifestations during the dedication. In early April 1836, Joseph and Oliver claimed that Jesus and ancient prophets Moses, Elias, and Elijah appeared and committed their priesthood "keys" to them in the Kirtland Temple.[1]

In November 1836, the Kirtland Safety Society Bank was established at the request of Joseph Jr. and other church leaders. Joseph believed the bank would reduce church debt, assist church members gathering in Kirtland, and strengthen the Kirtland economy. Joseph and other leaders served as administrators of the new banking institution. The plan was for the bank to issue banknotes as currency, thereby encouraging and expanding economic activity in Kirtland.[2] Samuel eagerly supported his brother's economic plans.

Meanwhile, in Missouri, the state legislature, led by Representative Alexander Doniphan of Clay County, created Caldwell and Daviess counties in December 1836. The purpose of creating these new counties was to resolve conflicts between church members and their neighbors by providing a place where expelled church members from Jackson County could resettle. It was expected that church members would settle in Caldwell County. However, church members quickly bought land and established settlements in Caldwell, Daviess, and neighboring counties. The largest settlement of church members was in the city of Far West in Caldwell County. A few years later, as many as five thousand church members lived in the county. They believed it was their constitutional right to settle wherever they wished, but acting on that belief proved to be an unwise move.[3]

CHAPTER 29

Panic and Loss

In March 1837, Mary and Samuel welcomed their second child, Mary Bailey. Mary's early years were marked with hardship. Her family was uprooted several times over the next seven years, and danger and death were constant threats. Despite this, Mary Bailey outlived her entire family before passing away well into the early twentieth century.[1]

Later that spring, the nationwide Panic of 1837 caused widespread bank failures across the United States. Historians typically attribute this economic crisis to a real estate bubble and erratic banking policies during the presidency of Andrew Jackson. The situation worsened considerably when President Jackson allowed the charter of the Bank of the United States to expire in 1836. The Panic of 1837 and the subsequent six-year depression had lasting effects on the American economy. In conjunction with declining land prices and the Kirtland bank's lack of a charter, the panic led to the closure of the Kirtland Safety Society Bank in the fall of 1837.[2]

Like most Americans, church members in Kirtland, including Joseph and Samuel, felt the economic hardship. Samuel personally "lost considerable money" in the Kirtland Safety Society Bank venture. Unsurprisingly, this led to tension and hostility among church members. Samuel must have been both angry and frustrated. However, there is no evidence that Samuel blamed Joseph or the bank for his financial losses.

Still, apostasy within the church became widespread. It is estimated that between 10 and 15 percent of the members in Kirtland left the church because of the banking crisis. Among those who left were the three witnesses to the Book of Mormon: Oliver Cowdery, David Whitmer, and Martin Harris, along with one of Joseph Smith's counselors, Frederick G. Williams, and four of the Twelve Apostles, John F. Boynton, Lyman E. Johnson, Luke S. Johnson, and William McLellin.

Additionally, many members of the Kirtland High Council became disillusioned. As a result, Joseph reorganized the council by appointing Samuel as its president.[3] Samuel certainly felt the pressure of leading the Kirtland community through these difficult times. Predictably, there were allegations of nefarious and illegal activities related to the banking venture, leading to legal actions against Joseph and others.[4]

Amid widespread discontent within the church and unrest in the community, many church members started leaving Kirtland for Missouri in December 1837. As the situation became untenable and their lives were clearly at risk, Joseph and other church leaders fled Kirtland on a difficult journey to Missouri. Samuel and his family also left Kirtland. He sensed the increasing opposition there and understood the potential consequences of staying.

During this turbulent time, Hyrum married his second wife, Mary Fielding, about two months after the death of his first wife, Jerusha Barden. Two months later, Sophronia also remarried, to her second husband, William McCleary, following the death of her first husband, Calvin W. Stoddard, about a year earlier.[5]

CHAPTER 30

Missouri and the Motto

Samuel and Mary settled in the city of Far West, Missouri, in early 1838. At that time, the town had over a hundred houses, several dry goods and grocery stores, blacksmith shops, two hotels, and schoolhouses. Far West was thriving.[1] For about the next year, Far West served as the church's headquarters.

Soon after Samuel's arrival, Joseph Jr. announced another revelation, which stated, "Let the city, Far West, be a holy and consecrated land unto me; and it shall be called most holy, for the ground upon which thou standest is holy. Therefore, I command you to build a house unto me, for the gathering together of my saints, that they may worship me."[2]

A site was dedicated and a cornerstone soon laid for a temple in Far West. In the same revelation that commanded the construction of a temple in Far West, the church's official name was declared to be "The Church of Jesus Christ of Latter Day Saints." Historical evidence suggests that this church name might have already been in use before this revelation.[3] Around that same time, in an effort led by Joseph, a political motto for the church was composed. It appears the motto was written in response to the church's expulsion from Jackson County and its conflicts in Kirtland.

The motto proclaimed:

The Constitution of our country formed by the Fathers of Liberty. Peace and good order in society Love to God and good will to man. All good and wholesome Law's; And virtue and truth above all things, and aristarchy, live forever. But wo to tyrants, mobs, aristocracy, anarchy and toryism, and all those who invent or seek out unrighteous and vexatious lawsuits under the pretext or color of law or office, either religious or political. Exalt the standard of Democracy! Down with that of Priestcraft, and let all the people say Amen! that the blood of our Fathers may not cry from the ground against us. Sacred is the Memory of that Blood which baught for us our liberty.[4]

The motto, written in a somewhat awkward and halting manner, may have been composed with Samuel's involvement. It is not entirely clear what Samuel's exact role was in developing the motto, or if he influenced any part of it. However, Joseph stated that "shortly after [Samuel's] arrival while walking with him & cirtain other bretheren the following sentiment [on the motto] occured to my mind." Samuel "attached his name to [the original] document" along with Joseph, Brigham Young, and a few others. From this document, it is clear that Samuel, Joseph, and the other signers regarded the US Constitution, democratic institutions, the Founding Fathers, and the American Revolution as sacrosanct. It is also evident that they had personal experience with and passionate feelings about mob rule, lawlessness, baseless lawsuits, and persecutions, as they explicitly condemned such actions in the motto.

Despite his support of the Constitution, Joseph did criticize it on one point five years later: "I am the greatest advocate of the Constitution of the United States there is on the earth. . . . The only fault I find with the Constitution is [that] . . . although it provides that all men shall enjoy religious freedom, yet it does not provide the manner by which that freedom can be preserved."[5]

Certainly, Samuel and his religious associates must have felt similarly; neither the Constitution, the United States government, nor local officials protected them from religious persecution. Samuel was about to experience this reality in the most personal way possible.

CHAPTER 31

Marrowbone Horror

Despite the thriving atmosphere in Far West, Samuel soon moved his family to the Marrowbone settlement about twenty miles to the northeast. Marrowbone, situated along Marrowbone Creek in Daviess County, had only recently been settled. Lucy Mack described it as a "desolate lonely place." Several other church settlements in Daviess County had already started, including one called Adam-ondi-Ahman, roughly fifteen miles north of Marrowbone. Presumably, Samuel either was asked or wanted to relocate his family to Marrowbone to advance and strengthen the church settlement in Daviess County. Samuel's physical prowess was certainly an asset in settling the barren landscape. A few months later, in early August 1838, Mary gave birth to her and Samuel's only son, Samuel Harrison Bailey Smith, at Marrowbone.[1]

Tensions and conflicts among church members, dissenters, and Missouri settlers persisted throughout the summer of 1838. Much of this unrest originated from disparaging comments made by dissenters who settled near Caldwell County. Church members also contributed significantly to the growing unrest. In response to rising tensions and the expulsion of the church from Jackson County, Missouri, and Kirtland, Ohio, church members formed an organization called the

"Danites" that summer. The Danites quickly gained an infamous reputation for intimidating dissenters and engaging in warfare against militias hostile to the church. Raids and looting were carried out by the Danites as well as by local settlers and militias. Joseph and other church leaders were aware of the Danite organization. Nevertheless, it remains unclear if they were aware of all the actions taken by the Danites.

According to scholar D. Michael Quinn, Samuel was a Danite.[2] Aside from serving as Joseph's bodyguard, presumably as a Danite, there is no evidence that Samuel participated in raids, looting, or clashes with Missouri settlers. Nonetheless, the events of the next few months would lead Samuel to defend his family and community.

Samuel Harrison Smith
Artist unknown, pre-1844

As skirmishes between church members and settlers in Daviess County mounted, Samuel traveled to Far West to get a wagon to relocate his family back to Far West, away from the tension and violence. During his absence, a mob broke into Samuel and Mary's home. Members of the mob carried Mary, her newly born son Samuel, and her young children Susanna and Mary out of the house on a featherbed while it was raining. The mob eventually burned down the home. A compassionate neighbor provided Mary and her children with a wagon and horses to travel to Far West to locate Samuel. An unidentified young man drove the wagon for Mary.

As Mary and the children traveled south toward Far West, they met Samuel along the way. Samuel's relief at meeting his wife and children on the road was quickly and grievously tempered as he was apprised of the trauma they had experienced. Thirty-six hours after Mary and the children left Marrowbone with little or no nourishment and drenched from the rain, Samuel arrived with his family at Far West, where his mother Lucy cared for them.

Decades later, Lucy recalled, "Every garment upon [Mary's] body, as well as her bed and bedding, was so wet with the rain that the water might been wrung from them. Mary was speechless and almost stiff with the cold and effects of her exposure." Mary never fully recovered from her ordeal. As a result of the trauma, it was said she never spoke above a whisper for the rest of her life.[3]

Samuel's resolve to protect his family and community naturally hardened. The distressing episode surely lit a fire within him. Samuel's instinctive response was to fight back.

CHAPTER 32

The Battle of Crooked River and the Flight

While in Far West, Samuel unsurprisingly joined a church militia of about seventy-five men led by Apostle David W. Patten. The Patten-led militia might have operated under the auspices of the Danite organization, although the Danites disbanded sometime during the fall of 1838. Arthur Millikin, a young convert to the church from Saco, Maine, was also part of the militia. Patten led his militia just beyond the border of Caldwell County into Ray County to rescue three church members whom a Missouri militia had taken as prisoners.

In the early morning hours of late October 1838, the church militia engaged a Ray County militia, commanded by Samuel Bogart, which had camped along the banks of Crooked River with the three prisoners. Both sides later blamed the other for starting the shooting. The battle, which became known as the Battle of Crooked River, lasted only about two minutes, but the firefight was intense during that short duration. Bogart's militia retreated. One of Bogart's militiamen was killed during the violent exchange. Further, three church members died from their injuries, and seven others were wounded but survived. One of the casualties was Apostle Patten. Patten has since been regarded as the first martyr of the Latter-day Saint faith. Samuel was not injured. After the Bogart-led militia retreated, church militia members rescued the three prisoners. They loaded them and their wounded into wagons and headed back to Far West.

The deadly conflict led Missouri Governor Lilburn Boggs to issue Missouri Executive Order 44, known as the "extermination order," which ordered the expulsion of the "Mormon" community from Missouri. A few days later, at Haun's Mill in Caldwell County, a militia attacked church members. The women and most of the children hid in the woods. The militiamen callously killed seventeen men and boys. Some surrendered and were killed execution style. Another twelve to fifteen were wounded.[1]

A different Missouri militia soon advanced on Far West. As it approached, Samuel and others quickly realized that if those involved in the Battle of Crooked River were discovered and captured, they could face execution. Samuel, along with others involved in the battle, fled Far West, heading north. The Missouri militia pursued them.

Early in their flight from Far West, Samuel asked those with him to consider what they should do if the militia caught them. They all agreed they would fight to the end. For Samuel and his fellow militia members, the fight to protect their families and community was deeply personal. Fortunately for these refugees, a snowstorm prevented the Missouri militia from tracking Samuel and his fellow militiamen. The refugee group eventually decided to split into three parties to avoid detection by any Missouri militia. After a few days, Samuel and his small group ran out of food. With the winter weather, options were limited. They finally resorted to eating slippery elm bark. In their desperate circumstances, the small group decided to pray for divine guidance. Leading the prayer, Samuel declared that their families were safe and that food would be forthcoming. Samuel's words proved to be prophetic. The next day, Samuel and his group found a Native American camp that provided bread and dried meat.

After a difficult trek, Samuel and his group finally crossed the Mississippi River and reached Quincy, Illinois, in November.[2] After an equally tough journey, Samuel's wife, children, parents, youngest sister Lucy, and brothers William and Don Carlos (with their families) arrived in Quincy about three months later. Samuel crossed the river himself and arranged a ferry ride for them to Quincy. He shared his rented house with his father and mother and helped nurse his mother and Lucy back to health.[3]

CHAPTER 33

Execution?

In November, Joseph Smith, his brother Hyrum, and several church leaders surrendered in or near Far West to Missouri State Militia Major General Samuel D. Lucas. The prisoners were placed in the custody of Brigadier General Alexander Doniphan's camp. Doniphan soon received an ominous, unsettling order from General Lucas, who ordered Doniphan to "take Joseph Smith and the other prisoners into the public square of Far West, and shoot them at 9 o'clock tomorrow morning."

General Doniphan responded promptly, "It is cold-blooded murder. I will not obey your order. My brigade shall march for Liberty tomorrow morning, at 8 o'clock; and if you execute these men, I will hold you responsible before an earthly tribunal, so help me God."

Saving Joseph and the other leaders, Doniphan took them to Liberty, Missouri, where they were imprisoned while awaiting trial in the spring on charges of treason. Meanwhile, church members used Far West as a staging ground for their departure from Missouri. Most traveled to Quincy, Illinois, and nearby areas. After five months of imprisonment at Liberty jail, Joseph and the others were allowed to escape and soon made their way to western Illinois.[1]

CHAPTER 34

The Macomb, Nauvoo, and Plymouth Years

As the Smith family settled in western Illinois in the spring of 1839, Samuel and Don Carlos accepted an offer from George Miller to farm land for him near Macomb, Illinois. The small town of Macomb had only been settled ten years earlier. George Miller, then a Presbyterian elder, reportedly joined the church several years later, after being healed from an unspecified malady, presumably by two church elders. Miller's compassion for church members crossing the river into Illinois from Missouri and his amicable relationship with Joseph Jr, Samuel, and Don Carlos may have facilitated his conversion.[1] Both Samuel's and Don Carlos's families lived on the farm for nearly two years. Since their wives were long-time friends and had suffered greatly in Missouri, it must have been a comfort for both families.

During this time, Joseph traveled with Elias Higbee, a former judge in Missouri, to Washington, DC, to seek compensation for their losses in Missouri. Joseph and Elias met with US President Martin Van Buren. According to Elias Higbee, President Van Buren responded to their request for help by saying, "What can I do? I can do nothing for you,- if I do anything, I shall come in contact with the whole State of Missouri."[2] Based on Elias's account of their meeting, Van Buren seemed most concerned about his political standing in Missouri. As a result, he did not offer or support compensation for the new religious movement. Unfortunately, there is no known written record from President Van Buren regarding his encounter with Joseph Smith or Elias Higbee. News of Van Buren's response to the church's request would have been a blow to Samuel and the rest of the church members.

As Samuel settled in Macomb, Joseph and Emma, along with their family, moved into a log home in Commerce, Illinois, located on the banks of the Mississippi River. Joseph directed the church to buy land throughout the small town. Church members worked to drain swamps, establish farms, build homes and roads, and start businesses. During this time, Joseph changed the name of Commerce to Nauvoo. In December 1840, Illinois granted a charter for the new city of Nauvoo that took effect in February 1841.[3]

Shortly after, in early 1841, Samuel and his family moved to Nauvoo. Samuel was quickly called to serve as a counselor in the Nauvoo bishopric. Several months before Samuel's move, the last of the Smith siblings married when Lucy, then nearly nineteen years old, married Arthur Millikin in Nauvoo.[4] Millikin had served with Samuel in the militia at the Battle of Crooked River about two years earlier.

In the fall of 1840, Joseph Jr. had discussed the doctrine of baptism for the dead while delivering a sermon at a funeral service. The idea of proxy baptisms on behalf of those who had died had been discussed at least two years earlier. Joseph argued that the practice was used by the early Christians during the time of the Apostle Paul, as referenced in Paul's epistle to the Corinthians in the New Testament.

He explained that this practice allowed those who didn't have the chance in life to hear Christ's gospel and be baptized to still attain salvation in the next life. The doctrine was quickly embraced by church members.[5]

During this time, Joseph Sr.'s health was declining. His dying wish was to ensure that a proxy baptism was performed for his oldest son, Alvin. Just before passing, Joseph Sr. blessed his children. To Samuel, Joseph pronounced, "you have been a faithful and obedient son. . . . The Lord has seen your diligence, and you are blessed, in that he has never chastised you. . . . these is a crown laid up for you, which shall grow brighter and brighter unto the perfect day." In September, Joseph Sr. died, apparently from the effects of the Missouri exodus.[6] Although there are no accounts of how Samuel responded to his father's death, as a father in his early thirties with three young children and another on the way, he must have been devastated. Still, his father's final blessing must have brought comfort. Samuel's young children may not have remembered their grandfather as they grew older.

In early January 1841, Mary gave birth to a daughter, Lucy Bailey. The situation quickly turned tragic. Samuel was grief-stricken when Mary died from complications during Lucy's delivery. Adding to his grief, his newborn Lucy died within a few weeks. Coping with the loss of his wife, his father, and his newborn daughter in less than five months was incredibly painful for Samuel.

In the face of this adversity, Samuel had three young children to care for and significant church responsibilities in the Nauvoo bishopric. Meanwhile, his civic responsibilities in Nauvoo continued to grow, as he was elected to the Nauvoo City Council and appointed as an associate judge of the

Nauvoo Municipal Court within a month of Mary's death. He was also named a regent of the newly established University of Nauvoo. Shortly after, he began serving as a guard in the Nauvoo Legion; Joseph was installed as lieutenant general of the Nauvoo Legion.[7]

In April, Samuel was called to serve another mission, this time in Scott County, Illinois. While there, he met Levira Clark, who was originally from Livonia, New York. It seems Levira was already a church member and may have met Samuel during a previous mission. Levira, described as a "mild, quiet woman," married Samuel within a month of his missionary assignment to Scott County. Samuel perhaps believed that his new marriage would reset his life. His young children were quickly moved to Scott County to live with Levira at her parents' home until Samuel finished his mission in November.[8] This must have been quite disorienting for Samuel's children, Susanna, Mary, and Samuel. The elder Samuel likely stayed with or visited Levira and his children often while serving his mission in the area.

During his time on the mission, Samuel's brother Don Carlos died of malaria. Sadly, malaria was one of the main causes of death in the Nauvoo community from 1839 to 1846.[9] This left his widow Agnes without her husband and close friend Mary for the first time since she had moved to Kirtland with Mary in 1833. Samuel completed his mission by November and returned to Nauvoo.

He then moved his family to the small village of Plymouth, Illinois, in early 1842. His brother William and William's family were living in Plymouth, which had been settled just eleven years earlier and was about forty miles southeast of Nauvoo. According to an early published history, other church members were also settling in Plymouth around this time. In Plymouth, Samuel and Levira helped William manage a tavern he had acquired a few years earlier. It is possible that the main reason Samuel moved to Plymouth was to support William's foray into politics. Samuel could run his tavern and manage other affairs while William ran for the state House of Representatives, on the Democratic ticket, hoping to win and serve as an advocate for the church in the Illinois House. William competed against Whig candidate Thomas Sharp to represent Hancock County. Sharp was becoming one of the most vocal opponents of the "Mormon" presence in Hancock County. William easily won the election and dedicated his efforts in the Illinois House to supporting and defending Nauvoo and its charter, which had been issued by the State of Illinois two years earlier. William served in the Illinois House from 1842–43.[10]

In April 1842, Samuel, along with his brothers Joseph and Hyrum and several church leaders, decided to declare bankruptcy. A new bankruptcy law, passed by the United States Congress in response to the nationwide Panic of 1837 and the ensuing depression, had just been enacted, allowing for voluntary bankruptcies. The law proved popular among those burdened by debt. Hoping to benefit from the more favorable terms of the new law, Samuel traveled with his brothers to Carthage to declare bankruptcy with the assistance of attorney Calvin A. Warren.[11] Although surviving records of Samuel's bankruptcy are limited, it was presumably approved by the Illinois District Court. This would have given Samuel significant financial relief.

During this same period, Levira gave birth to Levira Annette Clark Smith in Nauvoo.[12] Samuel's new wife and their newborn child might have helped ease some of the pain from the loss of his first wife Mary and their infant daughter Lucy around fifteen months earlier.

In 1843, Samuel acquired a farm just north of Plymouth. Throughout his residency in Plymouth and the surrounding area, Samuel enjoyed amicable relations with his neighbors, who regarded him as a "good" and "respectable citizen." In August, Levira gave birth to Lovisa Clark Smith in Nauvoo, but Lovisa soon died. Despite residing in the Plymouth area for nearly two years, Samuel often traveled to Nauvoo and was involved in civic and ecclesiastical responsibilities there. During the Plymouth years, Samuel served as a Nauvoo bishop, a City Council member, a member of the city's Committee of Improvement, and a Masonic Lodge member.

Even with his many responsibilities, Samuel still spent time with his children. As his daughter Mary later remembered, "Father would seat himself in the middle of the room. . . . the first on his lap got a kiss; so we would continue until we had all obtained the coveted kiss. . . . When we were all well tired out and quite sleepy . . . Father would take my brother—who was the youngest—in his lap, and sing him to sleep."

In December 1843, Samuel traveled to Nauvoo and received a new ordinance, called the endowment, in the upper room of Joseph's Red Brick Store. The endowment expanded upon the ceremonies administered in the Kirtland Temple years earlier, in which Samuel had been a participant. Joseph had instituted and administered this new ordinance at the Red Brick Store in Nauvoo since May 1842. Over the next two years, about sixty church members received this endowment ordinance, which included ceremonial washing and anointing. Members who received the endowment were called the "Anointed Quorum," or simply "the quorum."[13] The fact that Samuel received this ordinance demonstrated he was part of Joseph's relatively small inner circle. Eventually, Joseph wanted the endowment to be administered exclusively in the temple that was under construction in Nauvoo.

In late January 1844, church leaders gathered in Nauvoo for what may have been the most unique meeting in the history of the church. During this meeting, they discussed what actions to take in the upcoming presidential election. Everyone agreed that Joseph should run for president as an independent candidate.

Joseph publicly shared his reasons for running for the presidency: "I would not have suffered my name to have been used by my friends on any wise as president of the United States or candidate for that office if I and my friends could have had the privilege of enjoying our religious and civil rights as American citizens."

The apostles and over three hundred church members were called to serve missions to promote the church and Joseph's presidential campaign. They were instructed to present and distribute Joseph's platform as detailed in *General Smith's Views of the Powers and Policy of the Government of the United States*, which was published as a pamphlet. Thousands of copies of Joseph's campaign pamphlet were printed and distributed. Joseph's platform included a call for closing the country's expanding prison system, reducing the size of the House of Representatives, establishing a new national bank, and supporting national expansion conditioned upon receiving the consent of Native American tribes. Joseph also called for abolishing slavery in the United States through government action, using revenues generated from the sale of federal lands in the western United States to purchase the freedom of enslaved men and women from slave owners. Additionally, the church began publishing a newspaper in New York City called *The Prophet* that was dedicated to covering Joseph's candidacy and comparing his policies to those of other candidates.[14] It does not appear that Samuel was directly involved in his brother's presidential campaign, which lasted only about five months.

Samuel's brother William, one of the Twelve Apostles, was serving in the East during this time. During his service there in 1843 or 1844, William ordained recent convert Quack Walker Lewis, a free Black man from the Lowell, Massachusetts, area, as an elder. After Lewis was ordained, William and Lewis worked together for over a year in church service. It was clear that William was open to and embraced the Black community of his time.

Although there are no recorded statements about slavery or race from Samuel, one can infer from William's inclusive actions with Black parishioners that the African American community was supported in the church by Samuel and the rest of the Smith family. Additional evidence comes from Elijah Able. Able was an early African American convert to the church. He was baptized in 1832, ordained to the priesthood in 1836, received ordinances in the Kirtland Temple (which Joseph Jr. oversaw), and received his patriarchal blessing from Joseph Smith Sr. Moreover, Joseph and Emma shared their Nauvoo home with Jane Manning James, a free Black woman, who was also invited to be "adopted" into their family by priesthood sealing.[15] This early inclusivity did not survive the shift away from the Smith family's leading role in the church. In 1852, President Brigham Young restricted Black persons from priesthood ordinances, a ban that lasted until 1978. That policy history is one of many ways that the events set in motion by a pivotal decision made by Joseph in June 1844 have resounded ever since.[16]

Less than two months after Joseph launched his presidential campaign, he met with church leaders in the upper room of the Red Brick Store in Nauvoo. The discussion focused on settling areas outside what were then the boundaries of the United States. California, Oregon, and Texas were specifically mentioned as possible locations. Questions arose about how to plan and govern these new settlements.

As an extension of this discussion, they also deliberated on establishing a political kingdom or government in preparation for the millennial reign of Jesus Christ. An official council was organized for these purposes. Eventually, the council included fifty members. Joseph Smith intended for the council to operate separately from the church. While the church was responsible for handling spiritual matters and salvation, the council was a political or civic organization created to govern civil matters and protect the religious rights of all individuals, including those not affiliated with the church. As such, Joseph eventually admitted three individuals into the council who were not church members. The council was primarily governed by two parliamentary rules. First, the council could only convene when it had a quorum of at least 50 percent of its members in attendance. Second, the council only existed officially when it convened. Joseph stated that the council's name should be "The Kingdom of God and His Laws, with the Keys and Power thereof, and Judgment in the Hands of His Servants, Ahman Christ." However, the Council was generally referred to as the "Kingdom of God" or the "Council of Fifty."

Throughout its history, the Council of Fifty met only sporadically. Still, during its first three months in existence, the Council of Fifty was significantly involved in supporting Joseph's presidential campaign. About a month after the Council was organized, Samuel's brother William was admitted as a member.[17] Perhaps William's experience as a state legislator for the previous two years influenced his inclusion on the Council of Fifty.

CHAPTER 35

A Fateful Decision

While Samuel was maintaining his farm near Plymouth, Joseph and the Nauvoo City Council made a momentous decision in June 1844. Samuel had resigned from the City Council two years earlier. Around that same time, Joseph was appointed mayor of Nauvoo by the council. Mayor Smith and the council decided to shut down a new newspaper, the *Nauvoo Expositor*, and destroy its printing equipment. The *Nauvoo Expositor*, operated by former church members, had published only one issue, on June 7, 1844. That issue included a scathing, inflammatory criticism of Joseph Smith and the teachings he espoused that the publishers vehemently opposed, including plural marriage and the church's teaching on the nature of God. For William Law and the others who published the *Expositor*, it was a bold move.

Joseph and the council explained their reasons for their actions, calling the newspaper a public nuisance that posed a danger to the safety and well-being of Nauvoo. With memories of the violence church members had experienced in Ohio and Missouri still raw, and with tensions rising against the church in surrounding communities, they firmly believed the newspaper would incite further violence. A city shutting down a newspaper was not unprecedented in nineteenth-century America.

At that time, First Amendment protections only applied to actions by the federal government, not by states or cities. Still, the destruction of the *Nauvoo Expositor* intensified hostility in communities surrounding Nauvoo.

Vocal Latter-day Saint critic Thomas Sharp, who edited and published the *Warsaw Signal* newspaper downriver from Nauvoo, responded with an incendiary article about the destruction of the *Nauvoo Expositor*: "We have only to state, that this is sufficient! War and extermination is inevitable! Citizens ARISE, ONE and ALL!!!— Can you stand by, and suffer such INFERNAL DEVILS! to rob men of their property and rights, without avenging them. We have no time for comment, every man will make his own. Let it be made with POWDER and BALL!!!"

In hindsight, Joseph and the Nauvoo council made an ill-advised decision, the consequences of which quickly led to a catastrophic outcome. Even with the burgeoning turmoil in and around Nauvoo, had they responded to the blistering commentary of the *Nauvoo Expositor* by publishing a retort in a friendly newspaper and rallying support from Samuel in Plymouth and church members in nearby communities, they may have prevented the events that the destruction of the press unleashed. In that case, the accusations of tyranny and censorship within Nauvoo by church critics would have seemed unconvincing.

Soon after the press was destroyed, a judge in Carthage issued an arrest warrant for Joseph, Hyrum, and others involved in destroying the newspaper. The charge against them was inciting a riot. Illinois Governor Thomas Ford, fearing a larger conflict, assured Joseph they would be safe and receive a fair trial. After deciding not to flee to the Rocky Mountains,

Joseph, Hyrum, and the others surrendered. When they arrived in Carthage, Joseph, Hyrum, and Nauvoo City Council members were released on bail. Immediately upon their release, a charge of treason was filed and specifically directed against Joseph and Hyrum. They were then rearrested and taken to jail, where they remained, without bail, pending trial. The others were allowed to leave. A few chose to stay voluntarily with Joseph and Hyrum in the Carthage jail.

The mood in the jail was somber. Everyone knew their safety was uncertain. Sometime on June 26, church member John Fullmer visited Joseph at the jail and surreptitiously handed him a pistol. The next morning, church member Cyrus Wheelock visited Joseph and gave him a revolver. Joseph then passed the pistol he had received from Fullmer to Hyrum. By late afternoon on June 27, only Willard Richards and John Taylor remained in jail with Joseph and Hyrum. Shortly after 5:00 p.m. that day, a mob stormed the jail. In less than an hour, Joseph and Hyrum were dead.[1]

CHAPTER 36

Joseph, Hyrum, and Samuel

Early on June 27, Samuel learned that Joseph and Hyrum were imprisoned at Carthage and in danger. As quickly as he could, Samuel readied a team and wagon and headed to Carthage from his farm in Plymouth. He brought along a fourteen-year-old boy, who was working for him at the time, to drive the wagon. As they neared Carthage, members of the mob stopped them. Guarding the main roads into Carthage, the mob intended to stop anyone who could assist the prisoners. When they discovered Samuel's identity, they allowed the young boy to continue driving the wagon to Carthage but did not permit Samuel to proceed.

Just before fleeing into the woods, Samuel instructed the young boy to go directly to the Hamilton Hotel in Carthage and wait there. Alternately running and walking the miles-long journey back to Plymouth as fast as he could, Samuel eventually arrived at his farmhouse. Samuel's young daughter Mary remembered her father that day coming "into the house in much excitement," saying, "I think I can break through the mob and get to Carthage."

Samuel quickly mounted a horse and headed back to Carthage, determined to help his brothers. Samuel's young son remembered his father that day "perfectly well seeing him ride away from our farm on this race horse." As he neared Carthage, Samuel was told by a man and woman leaving the Carthage area in a buggy that Joseph Smith and the other prisoners had been killed. Shaken by the news, Samuel steadied himself and rode as quickly as he could to the jail. A couple of mob members hiding in bushes off the dirt road chased Samuel and fired shots at him with their rifles as he rode towards Carthage. Samuel quickly distanced himself from his pursuers and arrived at the jail. The mob had dispersed as soon as they determined Joseph was dead. Samuel was the first church member to arrive at the bloody scene.

One can only imagine the feelings of Samuel as he saw his brothers' lifeless bodies. Physically and emotionally drained and resigned to a pervading, deeply felt sadness and loss, Samuel navigated the next several hours with resolve. Samuel would have first seen Joseph's body outside the jail, lying against a well just below the second-story window from which he had fallen after being shot. The visual terror of the multiple wounds that had drained life from Joseph's body was inescapable. According to prison physician Dr. Thomas Barnes, Samuel carried the body of Joseph into the lower part of the jail. Climbing the stairs to the second-story room, Samuel saw his brother Hyrum lying on his back on the floor. The gruesome gunshot wound on the left side of his nose would most certainly have been seared into Samuel's memory as a perpetual nightmare. Soon after, Samuel and Willard Richards, who miraculously was unhurt during the fatal assault, moved Joseph and Hyrum's bodies to the Hamilton Hotel, located just a few blocks from the jail. Shortly after, Samuel, Richards, and a few others also moved the severely injured John Taylor to the hotel after Taylor had been attended to by Dr. Barnes.[1]

It is likely that if Samuel had managed to reach the Carthage jail earlier in the wagon, he would have arrived before his brothers' murders. In that case, Samuel probably would have been killed as well. No records show whether Samuel felt any guilt over not arriving in time to prevent their deaths. It certainly would not have been unusual for Samuel to experience such feelings, though, even if there was no merit in feeling that way. Decades later, Samuel's daughter Mary Bailey Smith Norman wrote that her father "did not fail in his efforts in behalf of his brothers in their greatest and last extremity. His failure to rescue them at Carthage was due to no fault of his own, but to uncontrollable circumstances."[2]

Perhaps Samuel had spoken to his wife, children, or others about feelings of regret or guilt regarding his brothers' deaths before he died. This could explain why his daughter felt compelled to defend her father's actions on that tragic day of June 27 decades later.

Willard Richards penned a letter to Emma that night from the Hamilton Hotel. The letter informed Emma that Joseph and Hyrum were dead. It also mentioned that John Taylor was injured. The letter was signed by Willard, John, and Samuel. Upon receiving the letter confirming Joseph and Hyrum's deaths, Emma was understandably devastated. She was also several months pregnant.

The next morning, Samuel, accompanied by Richards and eight guards provided by the state of Illinois, drove one of the two wagons carrying the bodies of Joseph and Hyrum to Nauvoo. Taylor would make the trip back to Nauvoo several days later. Lucy Mack saw the lifeless bodies of her two sons and "heard the sobs and groans of [her] family, and the cries of Father! Husband! Brothers! From the lips of their wives, children, brother, and sisters, it was too much, I sank back, crying to the Lord, in the agony of my soul, 'My God, my God, why has thou forsaken this family!'" The following morning, Joseph's and Hyrum's bodies were publicly displayed at the Mansion House in Nauvoo from early morning through the afternoon. Thousands viewed the deceased brothers. After the viewing, at just after 5:00 p.m. that same day, William W. Phelps gave the funeral sermon.

There were rumors and fears that Joseph's and Hyrum's bodies might be stolen or desecrated. Consequently, two coffins filled with sandbags were displayed at the funeral and given a mock burial at the Nauvoo Cemetery. Around midnight, the bodies of Joseph and Hyrum were hidden in the Nauvoo House. Without a doubt, Samuel would have been privy to these surreptitious activities to protect his brothers' dignity. Later, their bodies were covertly buried beneath a small outbuilding near Joseph and Emma's homestead.[3]

Samuel quickly moved with his family to Nauvoo. They occupied a two-story frame house across from the Mansion House. Levira was about six weeks away from giving birth.[4] Since Joseph had not publicly announced a clear succession plan, there was considerable confusion and apprehension among church members about who would succeed Joseph as the leader of the church. Anger over the murders of Joseph and Hyrum and uncertainty about the way forward caused a leadership crisis within the Nauvoo community. For Samuel and other members of the church, the murder of the founder, prophet, and leader of the religious movement they embraced seemed unfathomable. The additional title of martyr was now added to the religious pedigree of both Joseph and Hyrum, although the tragic distinction of Joseph being the first presidential candidate in United States history to be assassinated is rarely recognized. In addition to Joseph and Hyrum, the title of martyr would eventually be applied to another Smith brother.

Most of the Twelve Apostles were not in Nauvoo when Joseph and Hyrum were murdered. The church newspaper, *Times and Seasons*, announced on July 1 that no decision on succession would be made until the majority of the Twelve Apostles returned. Several names circulated throughout the Nauvoo community as potential successors to Joseph, among them Sidney Rigdon, a counselor to Joseph in the First Presidency, William Marks, Nauvoo stake president, and Joseph Smith III, Joseph's young son.

Samuel also was thought to be a potential successor. William Clayton, who was Joseph's recorder, scribe, and a member of his inner circle, recorded in his journal that Joseph had said that if "he [Joseph] and Hyrum were taken away, Samuel H. Smith would be his successor." Recognizing this, Clayton likely discussed Samuel as a viable successor with trusted individuals. Clayton also noted in his journal that Samuel, Willard Richards, John Smith, and William W. Phelps met on July 10 to discuss the issue of succession. The exact details of their discussion are unknown. Naturally, Samuel would have mentally and emotionally processed what the mantle of leadership meant for him and his family. It would have weighed heavily on him. Despite doubts about his abilities, Samuel always seemed willing to serve in any role necessary. There was enough speculation in Nauvoo about Samuel being Joseph's successor that an external newspaper, the *Sangamo Journal*, based in Springfield, Illinois, declared on July 25 that "a son of Joe Smith [Sr], it is said, had received the revelation that he was to be the successor to the prophet." Despite the newspaper's claim, there are no written records or documentation indicating that Samuel received a revelation to succeed his brother as President of the Church.

A few days after the July 10 meeting with Richards and Phelps, Samuel fell ill. In her account of Joseph Jr., Lucy Mack wrote that Samuel had complained just before his brothers' funeral service about "a dreadful distress in [his] side ever since [he] was chased by the [Carthage] mob, and [he thought he had] received some injury which [was] going to make [him] sick." By July 24, Samuel was very ill, and his health continued to decline.[5]

Samuel's daughter Mary Bailey, who was just seven years old at the time, recalled decades later that there was "a strange quiet pervading the house" during Samuel's sickness. "My sister, my brother and myself were banished to the room above with the injunction to keep quiet; our father was very sick. . . . Finally, for a day or two, we only went down to our meals; the tread in the sick room became more soft, the whispers more [soft], - then a silence save for sobs."[6]

On July 30, Samuel died. The shock of another death in the Smith family would have deepened the sense of foreboding both within the Smith family and the Nauvoo community at large. Samuel was thirty-six years old. His obituary was published in *Times and Seasons*. Samuel's cause of death was listed as bilious fever, but many later believed that he died from an unspecified injury sustained while being chased by the mob on his way to Carthage. His death narrowed the options for succession.

Samuel's widow Levira gave birth to Lucy Jane Clark just twenty days after his death. Lucy died within a few days of her birth. Being quite ill, Levira and her toddler moved back to her parents' house, leaving her stepchildren, Susanna, Mary, and Samuel, with Hyrum's widow, Mary Fielding Smith.[7]

Soon after his death, Samuel was likely buried in the Nauvoo Cemetery. Later, sometime after 1846, he was reinterred in what became known as the Smith Family Cemetery. The cemetery is situated just west of Joseph and Emma's homestead in Nauvoo. Today, Joseph Jr., Hyrum, Emma, and Samuel, along with twenty others, are buried there. However, fewer than half of the graves are marked. The graves of Joseph Jr., Hyrum, Emma, Joseph Sr., and Lucy Mack, along with a few others, are marked. Samuel's grave is unmarked, and it is unclear exactly where he is buried in the cemetery. Mary Bailey, Samuel's first wife, and their infant daughter Lucy, are also buried there, but their graves are unmarked as well.[8] Presumably, they are buried next to Samuel.

Samuel's burial site is overshadowed by that of his brothers, just as Samuel's role in church history has often gone unnoticed.

CHAPTER 37

Another Murder?

Amid shifting alliances during the succession crisis and fraught emotions stemming from the deaths of the three Smith brothers, tensions arose between members of the Smith family and church leaders. In the face of all the turmoil and tragedy, William soon concluded that his brother Samuel did not die from bilious fever but had been poisoned to prevent him from becoming Joseph's successor. According to William, church member and physician John M. Bernhisel told him that somehow anti-Mormons had poisoned Samuel. William also claimed that Levira told him that church member Hosea Stout was caring for Samuel and had administered "white powder" medicine. Perhaps William, recalling the tragic death of his oldest brother Alvin over twenty years earlier from the administering of calomel, was predisposed to frame Samuel's death in sinister terms.

Whatever William's reasons, he years later published his belief that Brigham Young and Willard Richards had ordered Samuel's murder by poisoning at the hands of Hosea Stout. Some later writers argued for the merit of William's murder theory by suggesting that Samuel opposed the practice of polygamy and that Brigham Young wanted to ensure that polygamy continued in the church. Although Samuel is not known to have practiced polygamy, there is no evidence that he was against the practice as taught by his brother. Indeed, strong circumstantial evidence suggests the opposite. William, for his part, did practice polygamy and publicly stated that he "was not ashamed of it [polygamy]" after his brothers' murders.

Notably, Joseph's widow Emma, who was known as a staunch opponent of polygamy, did not support either Samuel or William as her husband's successor. Instead of backing one of Joseph's surviving brothers, Emma actively advocated for William Marks, the Nauvoo stake president, to be her husband's successor. Marks was recognized as an opponent of polygamy.[1] This suggests that Emma understood that she could not count on either Samuel or William to oppose the practice of polygamy.

Many decades later, Mary Bailey Smith Norman, the daughter of Samuel and his first wife, wrote a letter to Ina Coolbrith, the daughter of Agnes Coolbrith, who was married to Samuel's brother Don Carlos. In the letter, dated 1908, Mary expressed her belief that "Father was undoubtedly poisoned" and claimed that "he spit out [the poison] and said he was poisoned. But it was too late- he died."

Mary Bailey was only seven years old when her father died, a tender age to fully understand such a situation. She did not claim to have witnessed these events personally; she implied that she was told about them and believed they happened. Given her age, it appears that her Uncle William was the source of her belief that her father had been murdered.

In the same letter, she told Ina that

Uncle Joseph ordained cousin Joseph- his oldest son as his successor- This done in Library Jail- He then

119

ordained Uncle William to hold the church for young Joseph until he was of age- but that last ordination was not done in public – Uncle William told me about this himself- He told Uncle William to hold the church together if he could But if he were unable to do so he should have the right to organize a branch if it were on an island in the middle of the ocean. After my father's death Uncle William considered his rights and claimed them.[2]

This letter clearly shows that Mary's Uncle William had a profound influence on her thoughts and beliefs regarding questions of succession. Interestingly, William initially supported Brigham Young and the Twelve as successors and later supported others as successors. If there were any truth to what William told Mary Bailey, he likely would not have supported Brigham Young and the Twelve or any other claimants as successors. According to Mary Bailey, William claimed his right to "hold the church together" until his nephew Joseph III was of age, asserting that he was ordained by Joseph for this purpose. Strangely, Mary Bailey "prepared a long statement, 24 June 1914, for the LDS Church Historian to whom she described [her father's] death without a hint of foul play." Scholar D. Michael Quinn argued that "this suggests that the Smith family in Utah kept to themselves their suspicion of Samuel's murder."[3]

Despite Quinn's solid credentials as a historian and his undeniable impact on Latter-day Saint scholarship, the evidence suggests a more nuanced conclusion regarding the murder question. Besides William Smith and Mary Bailey, there is no evidence that any members of the immediate or extended Smith family (no matter what their relationship to the church) believed he was poisoned. Furthermore, it is clear that William significantly influenced his niece, Mary Bailey. Mary Bailey accepted other claims made by her Uncle William that are probably false. The best explanation for Mary's reticence, assuming she did continue to believe her father was murdered, is that she did not want to make her views problematic or uncomfortable for her brother or other relatives in Utah. She ultimately moved to Salt Lake City later in life, was rebaptized into the church, and is buried in the Salt Lake City Cemetery.[4]

Unsurprisingly, Brigham Young heard about William's claim of his complicity in Samuel's death. On July 26, 1857, Brigham publicly stated that "William Smith has asserted that I was the cause of the death of his brother Samuel, when brother Woodruff, who is here today, knows that we were waiting at the depot in Boston to take passage east at the very time when Joseph and Hyrum were killed. . . . In a few weeks after, Samuel Smith died, and I am blamed as the cause of his death."[5]

Indeed, Brigham did not return to Nauvoo until August 6, six days after Samuel died.[6] Furthermore, it seems highly improbable that Brigham Young and/or Willard Richards could have known that Joseph's and Hyrum's deaths were imminent (and thus would lead to a succession crisis) and somehow planned Samuel's death while Young was away on a church mission. Nor does it seem probable that Brigham and William knew Samuel would become ill, thereby facilitating the opportunity for Hosea Stout to administer "medicine." There is no specific allegation, even from William Smith, that poisoning occurred before Samuel fell ill, as William specifically claimed that Hosea Stout poisoned Samuel *after* Samuel became sick. Such a theory strains credulity, as it assumes all these circumstances aligned perfectly so that Brigham Young could orchestrate a plot to become President of the Church at the expense of another claimant who opposed polygamy. Besides, as mentioned earlier, it appears that Samuel accepted polygamy as taught by his brother. Moreover, none of the other potential successors to Joseph died during that period, including those who opposed the principle of polygamy.

Samuel's wife at the time of his death, Levira, traveled west to Utah in 1851. Her move to Utah suggests she did not believe Samuel was poisoned or was the victim of foul play, at least not by church leaders. Levira married Dustin Amy, who also traveled to Utah in 1851 and married additional wives while still married to Levira. It is unlikely Levira would have participated in a polygamist marriage if Samuel had opposed the practice.

Additionally, Mary Bailey's brother, Samuel Harrison Bailey, who was just one year younger than her, did not believe their father had been murdered. Samuel Harrison Bailey Smith moved to Utah and remained a faithful member of the church under Brigham Young, even serving a mission. Samuel's son also practiced polygamy, a seemingly unlikely development had he believed his father opposed it and was killed for opposing it. Ultimately, two of Samuel's four surviving children, Samuel Harrison Bailey Smith and Levira Annette Clark Smith, relocated to Utah.

Furthermore, Lucy Mack did not seem to believe her son had been murdered. As noted, she remembered Samuel talking about an injury he had sustained while fleeing the Carthage mob. While Lucy Mack believed church leadership should stay within the family, she nevertheless spoke at a general conference before most church members moved to the

Salt Lake Valley, thus becoming the first woman to speak at a church conference.[7]

Samuel Harrison Bailey Smith
Photographer: C.R. Savage
Courtesy of the Church History Library

Levira Annette Clark Smith
Photographer: Edward Martin, ca. 1867
Courtesy of the Church History Library

Samuel Harrison Bailey Smith and Mary Bailey Smith Norman Grave Sites
Salt Lake City Cemetery, 2025

Other theories about Samuel's death have been put forth. One that "persists among some of Samuel's descendants . . . [is] that he suffered from alcoholism."[8] Another family tradition "holds that several days prior to traveling to Carthage, Samuel fell on a pointed object while working on the farm, and the accident created a hernia. Several days later, according to this tradition, as Samuel was attempting to outrun his pursuers while heading to Carthage, he leaned over the pommel of the saddle, causing his hernia to rupture and bleed. This internal bleeding increased until the time of his death."[9]

In the final conclusion, it seems very likely that he died from bilious fever or from an illness or injury that was not properly understood or diagnosed. Medicine in the early nineteenth century often lacked the precision needed to diagnose conditions accurately.

Had it not been for his untimely death, Samuel likely would have assumed the mantle of prophet and leader of the fledgling church, and he likely would have done so with the backing of Brigham Young and other leaders who were not part of the extended Smith family. During the last several years of his life, at least, Joseph clearly embraced the concepts of birthright and lineal descent. Consequently, Joseph envisioned his sons and family members assuming leadership roles in the church. Brigham Young and the Twelve Apostles appeared to support these ideas. Neither Joseph nor any of the apostles viewed the leadership role of the Twelve Apostles and the concept of a Smith family birthright and lineal descent as necessarily incompatible. Both, in their minds, could coexist. As such, Samuel was certainly a viable successor to Joseph, especially in the eyes of Brigham Young and the apostles.

Without a doubt, Brigham Young and the Twelve Apostles held great respect for the Smith family and their role as the "restoration family." Consequently, Brigham ensured that Lucy Mack was cared for during her final years in Nauvoo. Samuel's older sister Katharine faced severe poverty after the church moved to Utah. Brigham frequently sent money to Katharine to assist with her needs, even though he was aware that she had become associated with the Reorganized Church of Jesus Christ of Latter Day Saints, which claimed succession to Joseph's theology and church. Even years after leading church members to Utah, Brigham Young discussed the potential for Joseph's sons to take on leadership roles within the church, including serving as President of the Church. However, Young made it clear they would need to be worthy and accept the church doctrines as taught and established by their father.[10] Joseph III, was eleven years old when his father died. Emma also had their last child, David Hyrum, about five months after Joseph's murder. Since neither Joseph and Emma's children nor Samuel's surviving siblings moved west, church leadership was highly unlikely for them within the church, which was now based in Salt Lake City.

EPILOGUE

Matriarch Lucy Mack and her remaining children lost not only Joseph and Hyrum but also Samuel. All three sons and brothers were gone within thirty-four days. During his lifetime, Samuel endured the loss of his father and five siblings, his first wife Mary Bailey and one of their children, and another child with his second wife, Levira Clark. Still another child passed away shortly after Samuel's death. Death was never far from Samuel or his family. In addition to the constant specter of death, Samuel and his family encountered tremendous hardships.

Yet, despite their challenging journey through life, this rural American family in the early days of a new nation made a profound impact on the story and religious life of the United States and the world. No one familiar with Samuel's or his family's history can deny the significant role Samuel played in his family or the social and religious impact created by the Smith family from its roots in the small farming community of Tunbridge, Vermont. Thus, Samuel's life embodies a true American story; it is both a narrative of the "common man" and a story filled with distinction.

Samuel, the farmer from Vermont, lived in various places, including New Hampshire, New York, Ohio, Missouri, and

126

Illinois. He resided in frontier settlements, small villages, and townships, participating in many of the defining currents of the young nation. He faced the challenges of rural life, frontier justice, social and political strife, and religious revivalism and conflict.

Samuel was a hard-working man who lived a life of purpose. His daughter Mary remembered him working the farm "every day and part of every moonlight night." Samuel loved his family. He supported his parents, brothers, sisters, and religious community during the most difficult times. Even in dangerous circumstances, Samuel bravely risked his life to assist his family and advance his faith. As a humble man, he often played a supportive role, allowing others to succeed. He was a workhorse, not a show horse. Samuel was a devoted husband and father. He enjoyed interacting with and showing affection toward his wife and children. Sometimes, Samuel felt discouraged and aware of his shortcomings, as he acknowledged in his missionary journal. His family and close associates sometimes noted his unlettered persona and lack of eloquence, especially when compared to his brothers. Nevertheless, Samuel's physical presence, moral bearing, and sincerity resonated with his family, associates, and those he met. Rarely was Samuel petty, antagonistic, or prone to jealousy or anger.

Samuel's religiosity was consistently evident and never contained a hint of hypocrisy. Samuel faithfully served in various church and community roles, including serving on the Kirtland High Council and the Nauvoo City Council as well as in the Nauvoo bishopric and the Nauvoo Legion. He also served as a regent for Nauvoo University. Furthermore, Samuel introduced Oliver Cowdery to his brother Joseph, worked on his brother's farm to facilitate the translation of the gold plates, became the third person baptized in his brother's religious movement, served as one of the eight witnesses to the gold plates, was one of six charter members of the new church, and served as the first official missionary of the church. He accepted the call to serve six missions, traveling thousands of miles across much of the United States and establishing church branches in many states. He converted many people and was instrumental in converting Brigham Young and other consequential future leaders. Samuel also helped construct the Kirtland Temple and likely would have succeeded Joseph as the prophet-leader of the new faith if not for his untimely death.

Samuel's service was genuine and selfless. Although he experienced and achieved much, Samuel never exaggerated "either his importance or his experiences."[1] As such, Samuel was truly the quintessential son, brother, friend, and servant. Many also consider Samuel worthy of the title of martyr.

Although Samuel was a vital member of the Smith family, he was and has continued to be frequently overshadowed by his older brothers and the events that followed the founding of The Church of Jesus Christ of Latter-day Saints. Still, Samuel's impact was considerable. Therefore, the life of Samuel Harrison Smith should not be forgotten. The Smith family, initially divided religiously, was brought together as one, but then divided again as death claimed the three Smith brothers. Some members of the extended Smith family migrated to Salt Lake City and accepted Brigham Young as Joseph Smith's successor, while others did not. Some became affiliated with different movements or churches that claimed Joseph Smith's mantle, while others aligned with different

Christian denominations. Yet there is little to no disagreement or controversy about Samuel's life and his contributions to this influential new religious movement. Amid the tragic events involving the Smith family, especially in Samuel Smith's life, lies an enduring legacy.

Some people view The Church of Jesus Christ of Latter-day Saints negatively, and some views are quite hostile. Others see the Latter-day Saints in a positive light. As of this writing, membership in The Church of Jesus Christ of Latter-day Saints, based in Salt Lake City, Utah, exceeds seventeen million worldwide, with over 30,000 congregations. As the fourth-largest denomination in the United States, the church has nearly seven million members and approximately 15,000 congregations. Additionally, there are currently 367 church temples that are operating, under construction, or in the planning stages on every continent except Antarctica.[2] The Community of Christ Church (formerly the Reorganized Church of Jesus Christ of Latter Day Saints), headquartered in Independence, Missouri, has a membership of 250,000 in more than sixty countries.[3] Followers of numerous other movements and churches that trace their origins to Joseph Smith number in the tens of thousands. In 2016, the Library of Congress conducted an online poll in which the public chose the Book of Mormon as the fourth most influential piece of American literature.[4] In 2023, the Book of Mormon ranked as the sixth most published book in the world.[5]

Few, if any, religious movements that originated in the United States have had such a significant impact both nationally and globally as the Restorationist movement that became popularly known as the Mormon Church and is officially known as The Church of Jesus Christ of the Latter-day Saints.

Yet it started with an unassuming rural farming family, and one of its foundational figures was Samuel Harrison Smith, the other son, the other brother.

NOTES

Prologue

1. Thomas Villers, "Tunbridge Vermont State Soil," accessed August 30, 2025, https://www.soils4teachers.org/files/s4t/k12outreach/vt-state-soil-booklet.pdf.
2. "Mammals," Vermont Fish & Wildlife Department, accessed August 30, 2025, https://vtfishandwildlife.com/learn-more/vermont-critters/mammals.
3. "White River Wildlife Management Area," Vermont Fish & Wildlife Department, accessed August 30, 2025, https://anrmaps.vermont.gov/websites/wma/maps/White%20River.pdf. *White River Tactical Basin Plan* (Vermont Agency of Natural Resources, July 2013), https://dec.vermont.gov/sites/dec/files/wsm/mapp/docs/pl_WhiteRiverTacticalPlan.pdf.
4. Hamilton Child, *Gazetteer of Orange County Vt. 1762–1888, History of the Town of Tunbridge, Syracuse, N.Y.* (The Syracuse Journal Company, Printers and Binders, 1888).
5. Gary J. Aichele, "The Making of the Vermont Constitution: 1777–1824," *Vermont History: The Proceedings of the Vermont Historical Society*, vol. 56, no. 3 (Summer 1988): 137–90, https://vermonthistory.org/journal/misc/MakingVermontConstitution.pdf. *Tunbridge Town Plan* (Tunbridge Planning Commission, December 10, 2020), 11–12, https://tunbridgevt.org/wp-content/uploads/2021/01/Tunbridge-Transmittal-Draft-w-maps-2020.pdf.
6. "Historical Census Municipal Population Counts 1791–2020," VT Open Geodata Portal, https://geodata.vermont.gov/datasets/84a286c51ece48488273710e1f49834e/explore.
7. "The Family of Joseph Smith Sr. and Lucy Mack Smith: The First Family of the Restoration," *Ensign*, December 2005, https://www.churchofjesuschrist.org/study/ensign/2005/12/family-of-joseph-smith-sr-and-lucy-mack-smith-the-first-family-of-the-restoration.
8. John Sweeney Jr., "Biography of Samuel H. Smith to 1840" (Thesis, Brigham Young University, 1972).
9. Richard S. Van Wagoner, *Natural Born Seer: Joseph Smith, American Prophet, 1805–1830* (Smith Pettit Foundation, 2016), 21, 198, 334.
10. "Historical Census Municipal Population Counts 1791–2020."
11. "United States Population Chart," SUNY OER Services, accessed August 30, 2025, https://courses.lumenlearning.com/suny-ushistory1ay/chapter/united-states-population-chart/.
12. "The Louisiana Purchase: Jefferson's Constitutional Gamble," National Constitution Center, October 20, 2023, https://constitutioncenter.org/blog/the-louisiana-purchase-jeffersons-constitutional-gamble.

13. "Louisiana Purchase," *History.com*, accessed August 30, 2025, https://www.history.com/topics/19th-century/louisiana-purchase.
14. Linda Darus Clark, "Lewis & Clark Expedition," National Archives, accessed August 30, 2025, https://www.archives.gov/education/lessons/lewis-clark#background.
15. "Rural Life in the Late 19th Century," Library of Congress, accessed August 30, 2025, https://www.loc.gov/classroom-materials/united-states-history-primary-source-timeline/rise-of-industrial-america-1876-1900/rural-life-in-late-19th-century/.
16. Jenny Bourne, "Slavery in the United States," Economic History Association, accessed August 30, 2025, https://eh.net/encyclopedia/slavery-in-the-united-states/.
17. Alexander Von Hoffman and John Felkner, "The Historical Origins and Causes of Urban Decentralization in the United States," Joint Center for Housing Studies, Harvard University, January 2002, 3, https://www.jchs.harvard.edu/sites/default/files/media/imp/von_hoffman_w02-1.pdf.
18. "Growth of Cities," Digital History, 2021, https://www.digitalhistory.uh.edu/disp_textbook.cfm?smtid=2&psid=3514.
19. Stanley Lebergott, "Labor Force and Employment, 1800–1960," in *Output, Employment, and Productivity in the United States After 1800*, ed. Dorothy S. Brady (National Bureau of Economic Research, 1966), https://www.nber.org/system/files/chapters/c1567/c1567.pdf.
20. Jeremy Atack, et al., "Industrialization and Urbanization in Nineteenth-Century America," *Regional Science and Urban Economics* 94 (May 2022), https://doi.org/10.1016/j.regsciurbeco.2021.103678.
21. Pamela Riney-Kehrberg, "Farm Boys," Iowa State University Digital Repository, accessed August 30, 2025, https://dr.lib.iastate.edu/server/api/core/bitstreams/ec1227bc-2fc6-471e-94a9-3024dbdd5e3a/content.

Chapter 1

1. Richard Lyman Bushman, *Joseph Smith: Rough Stone Rolling* (Knopf, 2005), 12–13. "The Early Mack Family in Gilsum, NH," Joseph Smith Sr. and Lucy Mack Smith Family Organization, accessed August 30, 2025, https://josephsmithsr.org/wp-content/uploads/2023/10/Mack-Family-in-Gilsum.pdf.
2. Bushman, *Rough Stone Rolling*, 14–17.
3. Lucy M. Smith, *The Revised and Enhanced History of Joseph Smith by His Mother*, ed. Scot Facer Proctor and Maurine Jenson Proctor (Bookcraft, 1996), 39–43.

Chapter 2

1. Smith, *Revised and Enhanced History of Joseph Smith by His Mother*, 44–46.
2. Bushman, *Rough Stone Rolling*, 18.
3. Smith, *Revised and Enhanced History of Joseph Smith by His Mother*, 47–50.
4. Bushman, *Joseph Smith*, 18–19.
5. Smith, *Revised and Enhanced History of Joseph Smith by His Mother*, 58–61.
6. Smith, *Revised and Enhanced History of Joseph Smith by His Mother*, 62–67.

Chapter 3

1. Smith, *Revised and Enhanced History of Joseph Smith by His Mother*, 63–64.
2. James MacGregor Burns, *Fire and Light: How the Enlightenment Transformed Our World* (Thomas Dunne Books, St. Martin's Griffin, 2013), 86. Thomas S. Kidd, *America's Religious History: Faith, Politics, and the Shaping of a Nation* (Zondervan Academic, 2019), 54–55, 60.
3. Smith, *Revised and Enhanced History of Joseph Smith by His Mother*, 58.
4. Kidd, *America's Religious History*, 54–55.

5. Roger Finke and Rodney Stark, "Turning Pews into People: Estimating 19th Century Church Membership," *Journal for the Scientific Study of Religion* 25, no. 2 (June 1986): 180–92.
6. D. Michael Quinn, *Early Mormonism and the Magic World View*, rev. ed. (Signature Books, 1998), 223, e-book.
7. Quinn, *Early Mormonism*, 212.
8. Quinn, *Early Mormonism*, 23.
9. Quinn, *Early Mormonism*, 252.
10. Quinn, *Early Mormonism*, 254.

Chapter 4

1. "The War of 1812," Students of History, accessed August 30, 2025, https://www.studentsofhistory.com/war-of-1812-Timeline.
2. Mark Bushnell, "Then Again: Vermonters Were Bitterly Divided over the War of 1812," *vtdigger*, October 17, 2021, https://vtdigger.org/2021/10/17/then-again-vermonters-were-bitterly-divided-over-the-war-of-1812/. Edward Brynn, "Patterns of Dissent: Opposition to the War of 1812," *Vermont History: Proceedings of the Vermont Historical Society* 40, no. 1 (Winter 1972): 10–27.
3. Meghan Hamilton Morgan, "A Brief History of Conscription 1812–2002," TRACE: Tennessee Research and Creative Exchange, Spring 5-2002, https://trace.tennessee.edu/cgi/viewcontent.cgi?200breferer=200b&httpsredir=1&article=1580&context=utk_chanhonoproj.
4. "Ancestry of the Prophet Joseph Smith," Joseph Smith Foundation, accessed August 30, 2025, https://josephsmithfoundation.org/ancestry-of-the-prophet-joseph-smith/.

Chapter 5

1. Smith, *Revised and Enhanced History of Joseph Smith by His Mother*, 64–81, 91.
2. Dennis A. Wright and Geoffrey A. Wright, "The New England Common School Experience of Joseph Smith Jr., 1810–16," in *Regional Studies of Latter-day Saint Church History: The New England States*, ed. Donald Q. Cannon and Arnold K. Garr (Religious Studies Center, Brigham Young University, 2004), 239, 255.
3. Wright and Wright, "New England Common School Experience," 252–53.
4. Bushman, *Rough Stone Rolling*, 27.

Chapter 6

1. Smith, *Revised and Enhanced History of Joseph Smith by His Mother*, 82–86.
2. Bushman, *Rough Stone Rolling*, 31–33.
3. Spencer W. McBride, et al., *New York's Burned-Over District: A Documentary History* (Cornell University Press, 2023), 15–16, 21.
4. Bushman, *Rough Stone Rolling*, 37.
5. Bushman, *Rough Stone Rolling*, 37.

Chapter 7

1. Bushman, *Rough Stone Rolling*, 37.
2. History, circa June 1839–circa 1841 [Draft 2], p. 2, Joseph Smith Papers, accessed April 25, 2025, https://www.josephsmithpapers.org/paper-summary/history-circa-june-1839-circa-1841-draft-2/2.
3. J. W. Peterson, "Another Testimony, Statement of William Smith, Concerning Joseph the Prophet," *Deseret Evening News*, January 20, 1894, 11.

4. History, circa Summer 1832, p. 1, Joseph Smith Papers, accessed February 21, 2025, https://www.josephsmithpapers.org/paper-summary/history-circa-summer-1832/1.
5. History, circa Summer 1832, p. 1.
6. Quinn, *Early Mormonism*, 224.
7. History, circa June 1839–circa 1841 [Draft 2], p. 2.
8. James B. Allen, "The Significance of Joseph Smith's 'First Vision' in Mormon Thought," *Dialogue: A Journal of Mormon Thought* 1, no. 3 (1966): 29–46.
9. Bushman, *Rough Stone Rolling*, 39.
10. History, circa June 1839–circa 1841 [Draft 2], p. 2.
11. Chad Nielsen, "The Smith Family and the First Vision," *Times and Seasons*, June 25, 2022, http://archive.timesandseasons.org/2022/06/the-smith-family-and-the-first-vision/index.html.
12. Peterson, "Another Testimony, Statement of William Smith."
13. Nielsen, "The Smith Family and the First Vision."
14. Ruby K. Smith, *Mary Bailey* (Deseret Book, 1954), 15.

Chapter 8

1. "Monroe Doctrine," *History.com*, Accessed August 30, 2025, https://www.history.com/topics/19th-century/monroe-doctrine.

Chapter 9

1. History, circa June 1839–circa 1841 [Draft 2], p. 3, Joseph Smith Papers, accessed March 19, 2025, https://www.josephsmithpapers.org/paper-summary/history-circa-june-1839-circa-1841-draft-2/2.
2. Donald L. Enders, et al., "The Joseph Smith, Sr., Family: Farmers of the Genesee," in *Joseph Smith: The Prophet, The Man*, ed. Susan Easton Black and Charles D. Tate Jr. (Religious Studies Center, Brigham Young University, 1993), 213–25.
3. Bushman, *Rough Stone Rolling*, 31–32, 42.
4. Bushman, *Rough Stone Rolling*, 33, 42. Jacob W. Olmstead, "Life on the Smith Farm," The Church of Jesus Christ of Latter-day Saints, February 22, 2019, https://history.churchofjesuschrist.org/content/historic-sites/palmyra/life-on-the-smith-farm.
5. Quinn, *Early Mormonism*, 374–76.
6. Smith, *Revised and Enhanced History of Joseph Smith by His Mother*, 115–20.
7. Smith, *Revised and Enhanced History of Joseph Smith by His Mother*, 100.
8. E. D. Howe, *Mormonism Unvailed: Or, a Faithful Account of That Singular Imposition and Delusion, from Its Rise to the Present Time* (Published by the author, 1834), 240–41.
9. Smith, *Revised and Enhanced History of Joseph Smith by His Mother*, 124.
10. Quinn, *Early Mormonism*, 255.
11. Quinn, *Early Mormonism*, 321, 375.
12. History, circa June 1839–circa 1841 [Draft 2], p. 5, Joseph Smith Papers, accessed September 3, 2025, https://www.josephsmithpapers.org/paper-summary/history-circa-june-1839-circa-1841-draft-2/5.
13. History, circa June 1839–circa 1841 [Draft 2], p. 5. History, circa June 1839–circa 1841 [Draft 2], p. 6, Joseph Smith Papers, accessed March 20, 2025.
14. History, circa June 1839–circa 1841 [Draft 2], p. 7, Joseph Smith Papers, accessed March 20, 2025.
15. Smith, *Revised and Enhanced History of Joseph Smith by His Mother*, 112.

Chapter 10

1. Smith, *Revised and Enhanced History of Joseph Smith by His Mother*, 115–20.
2. Robert T. Divett, "Medicine and the Mormons: A Historical Perspective," *Dialogue: A Journal of Mormon Thought* 12, no. 3 (Fall 1979): 17.
3. Smith, *Revised and Enhanced History of Joseph Smith by His Mother*, 119.
4. Bushman, *Rough Stone Rolling*, 42.

Chapter 11

1. Smith, *Revised and Enhanced History of Joseph Smith by His Mother*, 124.
2. Smith, *Revised and Enhanced History of Joseph Smith by His Mother*, 124.
3. Linda King Newell and Valeen Tippetts Avery, *Mormon Enigma: Emma Hale Smith* (Doubleday & Company, 1984), 16.
4. Gordan A. Madsen, "Joseph Smith's 1826 Trial: The Legal Setting," *BYU Studies Quarterly* 30, issue 2, article 7 (April 1, 1990): 91–108.
5. Bushman, *Rough Stone Rolling*, 53–54.
6. "Hyrum Smith," FamilySearch, accessed August 30, 2025, https://ancestors. familysearch.org/en/KWJT-6XJ/hyrum-smith-1800-1844.
7. LaRene Porter Gaunt and Robert A. Smith, "Samuel H. Smith: Faithful Brother of Joseph and Hyrum," *Ensign*, August 2008, https://www. churchofjesuschrist.org/study/ensign/2008/08/samuel-h-smith-faithful-brother-of-joseph-and-hyrum. Mary Bailey Smith Norman, letter to Sue Smith Beatty, October 21, 1915, Harold B. Lee Library, Brigham Young University.

Chapter 12

1. Smith, *Revised and Enhanced History of Joseph Smith by His Mother*, 137–39.
2. Bushman, *Rough Stone Rolling*, 60–61. Smith, *Revised and Enhanced History of Joseph Smith by His Mother*, 148–50.
3. Larry E. Morris, "Empirical Witnesses of the Gold Plates," *Dialogue: A Journal of Mormon Thought* 52, no. 2 (Summer 2019): 59–84.
4. Steven C. Harper, "The Eleven Witnesses," in *The Coming Forth of the Book of Mormon: A Marvelous Work and a Wonder*, ed. Dannis L. Largey, et al. (Deseret Book, 2015), 117–32. Michael De Groote, "How Gold Were the Golden Plates?" *Deseret News*, July 7, 2010. Richard Lloyd Anderson, "Explaining Away the Book of Mormon Witnesses," FAIR, accessed August 30, 2025, https:// www.fairlatterdaysaints.org/conference/august-2004/explaining-away-the-book-of-mormon-witnesses. Howe, *Mormonism Unveiled*. William D. Russell, "Investigating the Investigation," review of *Investigating the Book of Mormon Witnesses*, by Richard Lloyd Anderson, *Dialogue: A Journal of Mormon Thought* 16, no. 2 (Summer 1983): 130–32. Fawn M. Brodie, *No Man Knows My History*, 2nd ed. (Vintage Books, 1995), 77–80.
5. Bushman, *Rough Stone Rolling*, 62–63.
6. Smith, *Revised and Enhanced History of Joseph Smith by His Mother*, 147.

Chapter 13

1. History, circa Summer 1832, p. 5, Joseph Smith Papers, accessed March 25, 2025, https://www.josephsmithpapers.org/paper-summary/history-circa-summer-1832/5#josephsmithpapers.
2. Bushman, *Rough Stone Rolling*, 64–65.

3. Smith, *Revised and Enhanced History of Joseph Smith by His Mother*, 160–66, 173–74. J. B. Haws, "The Lost 116 Pages Story," in *The Coming Forth of the Book of Mormon*, 81–102.

4. Smith, *Revised and Enhanced History of Joseph Smith by His Mother*, 161–62.

Chapter 14

1. Bushman, *Rough Stone Rolling*, 71.

2. Milton Vaughn Backman Jr. and James B. Allen, "Membership of Certain of Joseph Smith's Family in the Western Presbyterian Church in Palmyra," *BYU Studies Quarterly* 10, issue. 4, article 14 (October 10, 1970): 482–84.

3. Smith, *Revised and Enhanced History of Joseph Smith by His Mother*, 182.

4. Bushman, *Rough Stone Rolling*, 71.

5. Van Wagoner, *Natural Born Seer*, 334.

6. History, circa June 1839–circa 1841 [Draft 2], p. 17, Joseph Smith Papers, accessed September 23, 2025, https://www.josephsmithpapers.org/paper-summary/history-circa-june-1839-circa-1841-draft-2/23.

7. Smith, *Revised and Enhanced History of Joseph Smith by His Mother*, 182–83.

8. History, circa June 1839–circa 1841 [Draft 2], p. 19, Joseph Smith Papers, accessed March 25, 2025, https://www.josephsmithpapers.org/paper-summary/history-circa-june-1839-circa-1841-draft-2/25.

9. "Joseph Sr. and Lucy Mack Smith Family," The Church of Jesus Christ of Latter-day Saints, accessed August 30, 2025, https://www.churchofjesuschrist.org/study/history/topics/joseph-sr-and-lucy-mack-smith-family.

10. History, circa June 1839–circa 1841 [Draft 2], p. 19.

Chapter 15

1. Bushman, *Rough Stone Rolling*, 76.

2. Thomas F. Gordon, *Gazetteer of the State of New York: Comprehending Its Colonial History* (Published by the author, 1836).

3. Diedrich Willers, *Centennial Historical Sketch of the Town of Fayette, Seneca County, New York* (Press of W. F. Humphrey, 1900), 49. Ellen E. Dickinson, *New Light on Mormonism* (Funk & Wagnalls, 1885), 250.

4. Smith, *Revised and Enhanced History of Joseph Smith by His Mother*, 194–95.

5. Appendix 4: Testimony of Three Witnesses, Late June 1829, p. 589, Joseph Smith Papers, accessed September 4, 2025, https://www.josephsmithpapers.org/paper-summary/appendix-4-testimony-of-three-witnesses-late-june-1829/1.

6. History, circa June 1839–circa 1841 [Draft 2], p. 25, Joseph Smith Papers, accessed March 25, 2025, https://www.josephsmithpapers.org/paper-summary/history-circa-june-1839-circa-1841-draft-2/31.

7. Appendix 5: Testimony of Eight Witnesses, Late June 1829, p. 590, Joseph Smith Papers, accessed March 25, 2025, https://www.josephsmithpapers.org/paper-summary/appendix-5-testimony-of-eight-witnesses-late-june-1829/.

8. Smith, *Revised and Enhanced History of Joseph Smith by His Mother*, 201–03.

9. Bushman, *Rough Stone Rolling*, 80–83.

Chapter 16

1. Backman and Allen, "Membership of Certain of Joseph Smith's Family in the Western Presbyterian Church in Palmyra." Smith, *Revised and Enhanced History of Joseph Smith by His Mother*, 211–13.

2. Burns, *Fire and Light* 86. "The Age of the Common Man," Smithsonian American Art Museum, accessed August 30, 2025, https://americanexperience.

si.edu/historical-eras/colonization-revolution-and-new-nation/pair-daniel-lamotte-independence-squire-jack-porter/.
3. "Voting Rights Throughout United States History," National Geographic Society, 2025, https://web.archive.org/web/20220703214302/ttps://education. nationalgeographic.org/resource/voting-rights-throughout-history/.

Chapter 17

1. Bushman, *Rough Stone Rolling*, 109–10. Willers, *Centennial Historical Sketch of the Town of Fayette, Seneca County, New York*, 48. John E. Becker, *A History of the Village of Waterloo New York and Thesaurus of Related Facts* (Waterloo Library and Historical Society, 1949), 115. Don B. Taylor and Richard Bennett, "Samuel Harrison Smith, a Prophet's Brother," *Journal of Undergraduate Research* 2014, issue 1, article 1317, https://scholarsarchive.byu. edu/jur/vol2014/iss1/1317/. Gaunt and Smith, "Samuel H. Smith: Faithful Brother of Joseph and Hyrum."
2. Book of Commandments, 1833, p. 44, Joseph Smith Papers, accessed March 27, 2025, https://www.josephsmithpapers.org/paper-summary/book-of-commandments-1833/48.
3. Minutes, 9 June 1830, p. 1, Joseph Smith Papers, accessed March 27, 2025, https://www.josephsmithpapers.org/paper-summary/minutes-9-june-1830/1. Smith, *Revised and Enhanced History of Joseph Smith by His Mother*, 223–25.

Chapter 18

1. Smith, *Revised and Enhanced History of Joseph Smith by His Mother*, 225.
2. History, circa 1841, fair copy, p. 83, Joseph Smith Papers, accessed March 27, 2025, https://www.josephsmithpapers.org/paper-summary/ history-circa-1841-fair-copy/83?highlight=dust%20feet%20testimony.
3. Smith, *Revised and Enhanced History of Joseph Smith by His Mother*, 225.
4. Smith, *Revised and Enhanced History of Joseph Smith by His Mother*, 225, 244–246n2.
5. "Phineas Young's Account of Receiving Book of Mormon from Samuel Smith," *Church News* (archive), February 24, 2001, https://www.thechurchnews.com/2001 /2/24/23244824/phineas-youngs-account-of-receiving-book-of-mormon-from -samuel-smith/.

Chapter 19

1. Lyman D. Platt, "Members of The Church of Jesus Christ of Latter-day Saints Baptized by September 26, 1830," Ensign Peak Foundation, accessed August 30, 2025, https://ensignpeakfoundation.org/wp-content/uploads/2013/05/ NJ1_Platt4.pdf. Bushman, *Rough Stone Rolling*, 120–21.
2. William Chapin, *A Complete Reference Gazetteer of the United States of North America; Containing a General View of the United States* (W. Chapin and J. B. Taylor, 1839), 50.
3. Smith, *Revised and Enhanced History of Joseph Smith by His Mother*, 242–43.
4. Smith, *Revised and Enhanced History of Joseph Smith by His Mother*, 245–46. *History of Seneca Co. New York* (Everts, Ensign & Everts, 1876), 34n1–2. Larry C. Porter, *A Study of the Origins of The Church of Jesus Christ Latter-day Saints in the States of New York and Pennsylvania.* (BYU Studies, 2000), 104–05.
5. Dan Vogel ed., *Early Mormon Documents*, vol. 2 (Signature Books, 1998), 85. Bushman, *Rough Stone Rolling*, 42. Bruce I. Bustard, "Spirited Republic," *Prologue*, Winter 2014, https://www.archives.gov/files/publications/ prologue/2014/winter/spirited.pdf.

Chapter 20

1. "The Indian Removal Act and the Trail of Tears," *National Geographic*, accessed August 30, 2025, https://education.nationalgeographic.org/resource/indian-removal-act-and-trail-tears/.
2. Marlene C. Kettley, et al., *Mormon Thoroughfare: A History of the Church in Illinois, 1830–1839* (Religious Studies Center, Brigham Young University, 2006), 1–11.
3. Samuel Harrison Smith, Diary, 1832 February-1833 May, Typescript of diary, p. 11, Church History Library (The Church of Jesus Christ of Latter-day Saints).
4. "A Son of the Forest and an Intelligent Son of Abraham: Orson Hyde and Samuel Smith Meet William Apess, 1832," *Juvenile Instructor* (blog), November 21, 2013, https://juvenileinstructor.org/a-son-of-the-forest-and-an-intelligent-son-of-abraham-william-hyde-and-samuel-smith-meet-william-apess-1832/.

Chapter 21

1. Revelation, 2 January 1831 [D&C 38], p. 52, Joseph Smith Papers, accessed March 29, 2025, https://www.josephsmithpapers.org/paper-summary/revelation-2-january-1831-dc-38/4?highlight=the%20ohio. Bushman, *Rough Stone Rolling*, 122–25, 144.
2. "Younger, Katharine Smith," Joseph Smith Papers, accessed August 30, 2025, https://www.josephsmithpapers.org/person/katharine-smith-younger.
3. Bushman, *Rough Stone Rolling*, 144.
4. "Episode 6: An Endowment of Power," Joseph Smith Papers, accessed August 30, 2025, https://www.josephsmithpapers.org/articles/kirtland-city-of-revelation-podcast-episode-6-transcript.
5. Matt McBride, "Peter," A Century of Black Mormons, J. Willard Marriott Library, University of Utah, accessed August 30, 2025, https://exhibits.lib.utah.edu/s/century-of-black-mormons/page/peter.
6. Kyle R. Walker, *United by Faith: The Joseph Sr. and Lucy Mack Smith Family (Covenant Communications, 2005),* 213–14.
7. Bushman, *Rough Stone Rolling*, 155–56. Richard Henrie Morley, "The Life and Contributions of Isaac Morley" (Thesis, Brigham Young University, 1965), 19. Smith, *Revised and Enhanced History of Joseph Smith by His Mother*, 278.

Chapter 22

1. Minutes, circa 3–4 June 1831, p. 3, Joseph Smith Papers, accessed March 29, 2025, https://www.josephsmithpapers.org/paper-summary/minutes-circa-3-4-june-1831/1?highlight=conference%20kirtland%201831. Revelation, 6 June 1831, Symonds Rider Copy [D&C 52], p. 2, Joseph Smith Papers, accessed March 29, 2025, https://www.josephsmithpapers.org/paper-summary/revelation-6-june-1831-symonds-rider-copy-dc-52/2.
2. Kettley, *Mormon Thoroughfare*, 13–30. Smith, *Revised and Enhanced History of Joseph Smith by His Mother*, 278–80. Susan Easton Black, "Reynolds Cahoon," Doctrine and Covenants Central, accessed August 30, 2025, https://doctrineandcovenants central.org/people-of-the-dc/reynolds-cahoon/. Stella Cahoon Shurtleff, *Reynolds Cahoon and His Stalwart Sons: Utah Pioneers* (Paragon Press, 1960), 8–10.
3. Bushman, *Rough Stone Rolling*, 162–63. Shurtleff, *Reynolds Cahoon and His Stalwart Sons*, 11.
4. Smith, *Revised and Enhanced History of Joseph Smith by His Mother*, 294. Minutes, 25–26 October 1831, p. 10, Joseph Smith Papers, accessed March 29, 2025, https://www.josephsmithpapers.org/paper-summary/minutes-25-26-october-1831/1#historical-intro.

5. Revelation, 29 October 1831 [D&C 66], p. 10, Joseph Smith Papers, accessed March 29, 2025, https://www.josephsmithpapers.org/paper-summary/revelation-29-october-1831-dc-66/2.
6. Jan Shipps and John W. Welch, eds., *The Journals of William E. McLellin, 1831–1836* (BYU Studies and University of Illinois of Press, 1994), 66–67, 75, 300. Smith, *Mary Bailey*, 96. Revelation, 25 January 1832–A [D&C 75:1–22], p. 1, Joseph Smith Papers, accessed March 29, 2025, https://www.josephsmithpapers.org/paper-summary/revelation-25-january-1832-a-dc-751-22/1.

Chapter 23

1. Revelation, 25 January 1832–A [D&C 75:1–22], as Recorded in Hyde and Smith, Notebook, p. 28, Joseph Smith Papers, accessed March 29, 2025.
2. Samuel Harrison Smith, Diary, 1832 February–1833 May, Typescript of diary, 6, 9, Church History Library. Orson Hyde. Orson Hyde Journal, 1832 February–December, Typescript of journal, 12, 15, Church History Library.
3. Andrew Jenson, *Encyclopedic History of The Church of Jesus Christ of Latter-day Saints* (Deseret News Publishing Company, 1941), 211. "Missions of Samuel H. Smith," *Ensign*, August 2008, https://www.churchofjesuschrist.org/study/ensign/2008/08/samuel-h-smith-faithful-brother-of-joseph-and-hyrum/the-missions-of-samuel-h-smith.
4. Smith, *Revised and Enhanced History of Joseph Smith by His Mother*, 297–302. S. Kent Brown, et al., "The Joseph Smith Translation of the Bible: A Panel," in *Scriptures for the Modern World*, ed. Paul R. Cheesman and C. Wilfred Griggs (Religious Studies Center, Brigham Young University, 1984), 75–98.
5. Daniel Tyler, "Incidents of Experience," in *Scraps of Biography: Tenth Book of the Faith-Promoting Series* (Juvenile Instructor Office, 1883), 23–24.
6. Samuel Harrison Smith, Diary, 1832 February–1833 May, Typescript of diary, 8.
7. Samuel Harrison Smith, Diary, 1832 February–1833 May, Typescript of diary, 9, 21, 24, 26. Sweeney Jr., "Biography of Samuel H. Smith to 1840," 1–2.
8. *Millennial Star,* November 26, 1864. 774.
9. John A. Widtsoe, *Joseph Smith: Seeker After Truth, Prophet of God* (Deseret News Press, 1951), 166.
10. Samuel Harrison Smith, Diary, 1832 February-1832–1833 May, Typescript of diary, 8, 9.
11. Jeffrey D. Mahas, "Ball, Joseph T," A Century of Black Mormons, accessed August 30, 2025, https://exhibits.lib.utah.edu/s/century-of-black-mormons/page/ball-joseph-t#?xywh=-3376%2C-215%2C9260%2C4288.
12. Samuel Harrison Smith, Diary, 1832 February 1832–1833 May, Typescript of diary, 9, 10, 14. Smith, *Mary Bailey*, 10.
13. Smith, *Mary Bailey*, 31–32.
14. Smith, *Mary Bailey*, 30.
15. Smith, *Mary Bailey*, 38.
16. Samuel Harrison Smith, Diary, 1832 February 1832–1833 May, Typescript of diary, 10.
17. Samuel Harrison Smith, Diary, 1832 February 1832–1833 May, Typescript of diary, 17.
18. Samuel Harrison Smith, Diary, 1832 February 1832–1833 May, Typescript of diary, 4.
19. Samuel Harrison Smith, Diary, 1832 February 1832–1833 May, Typescript of diary, 12.
20. Samuel Harrison Smith, Diary, 1832 February 1832–1833 May, Typescript of diary, 12–13. Brent M. Rogers, "Vienna Jaques: Woman of Faith," *Ensign*, June 2016, https://www.churchofjesuschrist.org/study/ensign/2016/06/vienna-jaques-woman-of-faith.

21. Samuel Harrison Smith, Diary, 1832 February–1833 May, Typescript of diary, 20, 24. Orson Hyde, Orson Hyde Journal, 1832 February–December, Typescript of journal, 36–37, 39, Church History Library. "The Cochran Fanaticism in York County," *Maine History* 20, no. 1, article 3 (Maine Historical Society, 1980): 23–39. Nancy Ponzetti, "The Cochrane Craze," *BHHS Newsletter*, Buxton-Hollis Historical Society, Fall 2020.

22. "Joseph Smith/Polygamy/Cochranites," FAIR, accessed August 30, 2025, https:// www.fairlatterdaysaints.org/answers/Joseph_Smith/Polygamy/Cochranites.

23. Hendrik Hartog, "Marital Exits and Marital Expectations in Nineteenth Century America," Philip A. Hart Memorial Lecture, Georgetown University Law Center, April 10, 1991, https://scholarship.law.georgetown.edu/ hartlecture/8/. Elizabeth Dunn, "5 19th-Century Utopian Communities in the United States," *History.com*, accessed August 30, 2025. https://www.history. com/articles/5-19th-century-utopian-communities-in-the-united-states.. Richard S. Van Wagoner, "Mormon Polyandry in Nauvoo," *Dialogue: Journal of Mormon Thought* 18, no. 3 (Fall 1985): 67–83. Brian C. Hales, "Joseph Smith's Practice of Plural Marriage," BYU Religious Studies Center, accessed October 22, 2025, https://rsc.byu.edu/sites/default/files/pub_content/pdf/ Joseph_Smiths_Practice_of_Plural_Marraige.pdf.

24. Brian C. Hales, *Joseph Smith's Polygamy*, vol. 2: *History* (Greg Kofford Books, 2013), 42–47.

25. Samuel Harrison Smith, Diary, 1832 February–1833 May, Typescript of diary, 24–26. Orson Hyde, Orson Hyde Journal, Typescript of journal, 39, Church History Library.

26. Samuel Harrison Smith, Diary, 1832 February–1833 May, Typescript of diary, 29. Bushman, *Rough Stone Rolling*, 189. Smith, *Revised and Enhanced History of Joseph Smith by His Mother*, 307.

Chapter 24

1. Samuel Harrison Smith, Diary, 1832 February–1833 May, Typescript of diary, 29. Bushman, *Rough Stone Rolling*, 216–19.

2. Irene Bates, "William Smith, 1811–1893: Problematic Patriarch," *Dialogue: A Journal of Mormon Thought* 16, no. 2 (Summer 1983): 11–12.

3. Smith, *Mary Bailey*, 32–34.

4. Smith, *Revised and Enhanced History of Joseph Smith by His Mother*, 323. Bushman, *Rough Stone Rolling*, 216–18. Shaun D. Stahle, "Samuel H. Smith Honored by Family," *Church News* (archive), June 2005, https://www. thechurchnews.com/2005/6/18/23236436/samuel-h-smith-honored-by-family/.

5. Bushman, *Rough Stone Rolling*, 222–29. *Evening and Morning Star*, vol. 1–2, "Free People of Color," 218, https://contentdm.lib.byu.edu/digital/collection/ NCMP1820-1846/id/28024. Mary E. Rollins Lightner, "Ran from the Mob," *Deseret Evening News*, February 20, 1904, 24. Rogers, "Vienna Jaques: Woman of Faith." Wilford C. Wood, *Joseph Smith Begins His Work*, vol. 2 (Wilford C. Wood Publisher, 1962), 160.

6. "Church Officers in the Kirtland Stake, October 1835–January 1838," Joseph Smith Papers, accessed August 30, 205, https://www.josephsmithpapers.org/ back/church-officers-in-the-kirtland-stake-october-1835-january-1838.

7. Appendix 5, Document 3. Blessing to Samuel Smith, 28 September 1835, p. 10, Joseph Smith Papers, accessed April 1, 2025, https://www.josephsmithpapers.org/ paper-summary/appendix-5-document-3-blessing-to-samuel-smith-28-september -1835/1. History, 1838–1856, volume B-1 [1 September 1834–2 November 1838], p. 612, Joseph Smith Papers, accessed April 1, 2025, https://www. josephsmithpapers.org/paper-summary/history-1838-1856-volume-b-1-1- september-1834-2-november-1838/66.

8. "Zion's Camp (Camp of Israel)," The Church of Jesus Christ of Latter-day Saints, accessed August 30, 2025, https://www.churchofjesuschrist.org/study/history/topics/zions-camp-camp-of-israel.
9. Smith, *Revised and Enhanced History of Joseph Smith by His Mother*, 332n.

Chapter 25

1. "Patriarchal Blessings by Joseph Smith Sr.," December 9, 1834, accessed August 30, 2025, https://user.xmission.com/~research/mormonpdf/blessingsbyjssr.pdf.
2. Mary Bailey Smith, letter to Emma, December 23, 1834, in Joseph B. Smith Jr. Collection, Church History Library.

Chapter 26

1. Matthew C. Godfrey, "A Great Blessing: The Calling of the Original Twelve Apostles in This Dispensation," The Church of Jesus Christ of Latter-day Saints, accessed August 30, 2025, https://history.churchofjesuschrist.org/content/perspectives-on-church-history/a-great-blessing. Letter from William Smith, 18 December 1835, p. 79, Joseph Smith Papers, accessed April 1, 2025, https://www.josephsmithpapers.org/paper-summary/letter-from-william-smith-18-december-1835/3. William Smith, *William Smith on Mormonism: A True Account of the Origin of the Book of Mormon* (Herald Steam Book and Job Office, 1883), 10, 15.
2. "Joseph Sr. and Lucy Mack Smith Family," The Church of Jesus Christ of Latter-day Saints, accessed August 30, 2025, https://www.churchofjesuschrist.org/study/history/topics/joseph-sr-and-lucy-mack-smith-family.
3. "Doctrine and Covenants, 1835," Joseph Smith Papers, accessed August 30, 2025, https://www.josephsmithpapers.org/paper-summary/doctrine-and-covenants-1835/1.
4. "The Pearl of Great Price," Joseph Smith Papers, accessed August 30, 2025, https://www.josephsmithpapers.org/site/the-pearl-of-great-price.
5. Journal, 1835–1836, p. 9, Joseph Smith Papers, accessed April 1, 2025, https://www.josephsmithpapers.org/paper-summary/journal-1835-1836/10.
6. "Revelation, 27 October, 1835," Joseph Smith Papers, accessed August 30, 2025, https://www.josephsmithpapers.org/paper-summary/revelation-27-october-1835/1. Smith, *Mary Bailey*, 46.
7. Mary Bailey Smith, letter to Samuel, undated, in Joseph B. Smith Jr. Collection, Church History Library.

Chapter 27

1. Letter from William Smith, 18 December 1835. Brian Reeves, "'A Battle Ensued': John P. Greene and Samuel H. Smith in the Early Restoration," accessed August 30, 2025, http://young.parkinsonfamily.org/john/histories/jpg-samuel-smith.htm. Bates, "William Smith, 1811–1893: Problematic Patriarch," 13–14.

Chapter 28

1. History, 1838–1856, volume B-1 [1 September 1834–2 November 1838], p. 641, Joseph Smith Papers, accessed April 2, 2025, https://www.josephsmithpapers.org/paper-summary/history-1838-1856-volume-b-1-1-september-1834-2-november-1838/95. Bushman, *Rough Stone Rolling*, 308–21.
2. Bushman, *Rough Stone Rolling*, 328–32.
3. Bushman, *Rough Stone Rolling*, 342–46. "The History of Caldwell County," Caldwell County Commission, accessed August 20, 2025, https://www.caldwellco.missouri.org/about-and-history-of-caldwell-county/.

Chapter 29

1. "Mary Bailey Smith," FamilySearch, accessed August 30, 2025, https://ancestors.familysearch.org/en/L21G-6BL/mary-bailey-smith-.
2. "1837: The Hard Times," Harvard Business School, accessed August 30, 2025, https://www.library.hbs.edu/hc/crises/1837.html. "Nineteenth-Century Banking and the Financial Panic of 1837," Joseph Smith Papers, accessed August 30, 2025, https://www.josephsmithpapers.org/articles/financial-panic-of-1837.
3. "The Church Moves to Northern Missouri," The Church of Jesus Christ of Latter-day Saints, accessed August 30, 2025, https://www.churchofjesuschrist.org/study/manual/doctrine-and-covenants-and-church-history-seminary-teacher-manual-2014/section-6/lesson-121-the-church-moves-to-northern-missouri. Sweeney Jr., "Biography of Samuel H. Smith to 1840," 6. Smith, *Mary Bailey*, 60.
4. Jeffrey N. Walker, "The Kirtland Safety Society and the Fraud of Grandison Newell: A Legal Examination," *BYU Studies Quarterly* 54, issue. 3, article 5 (2015): 33–148.
5. Kettley, *Mormon Thoroughfare*, 79–94. "The Family of Joseph Smith Sr. and Lucy Mack Smith: The First Family of the Restoration."

Chapter 30

1. James B. Allen and Glen M. Leonard, *The Story of the Latter-day Saints* (1976; repr., Deseret Book, 1992), 116–17.
2. Revelation, 26 April 1838 [D&C 115], p. 33, Joseph Smith Papers, accessed April 3, 2025, https://www.josephsmithpapers.org/paper-summary/revelation-26-april-1838-dc-115/2.
3. Revelation, 26 April 1838 [D&C 115], p. 33. Bushman, *Rough Stone Rolling*, 338–39. Letter to the Church, circa April 1834, p. 152, Joseph Smith Papers, accessed April 3, 2025, https://www.josephsmithpapers.org/paper-summary/letter-to-the-church-circa-april-1834/1.
4. Motto, circa 16 or 17 March 1838, p. 16, Joseph Smith Papers, accessed April 3, 2025, https://www.josephsmithpapers.org/paper-summary/motto-circa-16-or-17-march-1838/1.
5. "Joseph Smith," in *Latter-day Prophets and the United States Constitution*, ed. Donald Q Cannon (Religious Studies Center, Brigham Young University, 1991), 1–13. Motto, circa 16 or 17 March 1838, p. 17, Joseph Smith Papers, accessed May 9, 2025, https://www.josephsmithpapers.org/paper-summary/motto-circa-16-or-17-march-1838/2.

Chapter 31

1. Smith, *Revised and Enhanced History of Joseph Smith by His Mother*, 364–65.
2. "Danites," Joseph Smith Papers.org, accessed August 30, 2025, https://www.josephsmithpapers.org/topic/danites. D. Michael Quinn, *The Mormon Hierarchy: Origins of Power* (Signature Books in association with Smith Research Associates, 1994), 93–103, 484.
3. Gaunt and Smith, "Samuel H. Smith: Faithful Brother of Joseph and Hyrum." Lucy Mack Smith, History, 1845, p. 251, Joseph Smith Papers, accessed April 3, 2025, https://www.josephsmithpapers.org/paper-summary/lucy-mack-smith-history-1845/259. Smith, *Revised and Enhanced History of Joseph Smith by His Mother*, 365.

Chapter 32

1. Mark Boardman, "Battle for the Promised Land," *True West: History of the American Frontier*, July 4, 2019, https://truewestmagazine.com/article/battle-for-the-promised-land/. Erin B. Metcalfe, "Firm and Steadfast in the Faith," *Mormon Historical Studies* 14, no. 2 (Fall 2013): 109–21. "Battle of Crooked River," Ray County Museum, accessed August 30, 2025, https://raycountymuseum.org/home/history/battle-of-crooked-river/. Gaunt and Smith, "Samuel H. Smith: Faithful Brother of Joseph and Hyrum." Alma R. Blair, "The Haun's Mill Massacre," *BYU Studies Quarterly* 13, issue. 1, article 8 (1973): 62–67, https://scholarsarchive.byu.edu/byusq/vol13/iss1/8. "Danites," The Church of Jesus Christ of Latter-day Saints, accessed August 30, 2025, https://www.churchofjesuschrist.org/study/history/topics/danites. Quinn, *Mormon Hierarchy*, 485.
2. Reeves, Brian. "'A Battle Ensured.'" Gaunt and Smith, "Samuel H. Smith: Faithful Brother of Joseph and Hyrum."
3. Smith, *Revised and Enhanced History of Joseph Smith by His Mother*, 418–19. Smith, *Mary Bailey*, 81.

Chapter 33

1. Bushman, *Rough Stone Rolling* 366–70, 382. Kimberly Harper, "Alexander W. Doniphan," Historic Missourians, accessed August 30, 2025, https://historicmissourians.shsmo.org/alexander-doniphan/.

Chapter 34

1. "Pay Order to Newel K. Whitney for George Miller, 18 September 1840," Joseph Smith Papers, accessed August 30, 2025, https://www.josephsmithpapers.org/paper-summary/pay-order-to-newel-k-whitney-for-george-miller-18-september-1840/1#historical-intro. S. J. Clarke, *History of McDonough County Illinois, Its Cities, Towns, and Villages with Early Reminiscences, Personal Incidents and Anecdotes* (D. W. Lusk, State Printer and Binder, 1878), 82–83, 309. "History of Macomb," Macomb Area Chamber of Commerce, accessed August 30, 2025, https://www.macombareachamber.com/history-of-macomb/.
2. Ronald O. Barney, "Joseph Smith Goes to Washington," in *Joseph Smith, the Prophet and Seer*, ed. Richard Neitzel Holzapfel and Kent P. Jackson (Deseret Book, 2010), 391–420.
3. Bushman, *Rough Stone Rolling*, 403–16.
4. "Church Officers in Nauvoo, Illinois, September 1842–February 1843," Joseph Smith Papers.org, accessed August 30, 2025, https://www.josephsmithpapers.org/back/church-officers-in-nauvoo-illinois-september-1842-february-1843. Gaunt and Smith, "Samuel H. Smith: Faithful Brother of Joseph and Hyrum." Marriage License and Certificate for Arthur Millikin and Lucy Smith, 3 June 1840, p. 1, Joseph Smith Papers, accessed April 4, 2025, https://www.josephsmithpapers.org/paper-summary/marriage-license-and-certificate-for-arthur-millikin-and-lucy-smith-3-june-1840/1.
5. Alexander L. Baugh, "For Their Salvation is Necessary and Essential to Our Salvation," in *An Eye of Faith: Essays in Honor of Richard O. Cowan*, ed. Kenneth L. Alford and Richard E. Bennett (Religious Studies Center, 2015), 113–37.
6. Smith, *Revised and Enhanced History of Joseph Smith by His Mother*, 431–37. Lawrence R. Flake, *Prophets and Apostles of the Last Dispensation* (Deseret Book, 2001), 307–10.
7. "Samuel H. Smith: Faithful Through Many Trials," Terrie Lynn Bittner, History of Mormonism, accessed August 30, 2025, https://historyofmormonism.com/2013/06/27/samuel-h-smith/. Minutes, 3 February 1841, Copy, p. 4, Joseph

Smith Papers, accessed April 4, 2025, https://www.josephsmithpapers.org/paper-summary/minutes-3february-1841-copy/4. "Nauvoo City Officers," Joseph Smith Papers, https://www.josephsmithpapers.org/back/nauvoo-city-officers-1841-1844. "Samuel Harrison Smith," Latter Day Light, accessed August 30, 2025, https://latterdaylight.com/samuel-harrison-smith/.

8. History, 1838–1856, volume F-1 [1 May 1844–8 August 1844], p. 292, Joseph Smith Papers, accessed April 4, 2025, https://www.josephsmithpapers.org/paper-summary/history-1838-1856-volume-f-1-1-may-1844-8-august-1844/299. Gaunt and Smith, "Samuel H. Smith: Faithful Brother of Joseph and Hyrum." Smith, *Mary Bailey*, 92.

9. Letter from John E. Page, 1 September 1841, p. 1, Joseph Smith Papers, accessed April 4, 2025, https://www.josephsmithpapers.org/paper-summary/letter-from-johne-page-1september-1841/6. Evan L. Ivie and Douglas C. Heiner, "Deaths in Early Nauvoo, Illinois, 1839–1846, and in Winter Quarters, Nebraska, 1846–48," *Religious Educator* 10, no. 3 (2009): 163–74.

10. Gaunt and Smith, "Samuel H. Smith: Faithful Brother of Joseph and Hyrum." E. H. Young, *A History of Round Prairie and Plymouth. 1831–1875* (Geo. J. Titus, Book and Job Printer, 1876), 64–66, 87. "Plymouth, Illinois," Joseph Smith Papers.org, accessed August 30, 2025, https://www.josephsmithpapers.org/place/plymouth-illinois. "Growing Conflict in Illinois," The Church of Jesus Christ of Latter-day Saints, accessed October 28, 2025, https://www.churchofjesuschrist.org/study/manual/church-history-in-the-fulness-of-times/chapter-twenty-one.

11. "Introduction to Joseph Smith's Bankruptcy," Joseph Smith Papers, accessed August 30, 2025, https://www.josephsmithpapers.org/paper-summary/introduction-to-joseph-smiths-bankruptcy/1.

12. "Levira Annette Clark Smith," The Church of Jesus Christ of Latter-day Saints, Church Historical Database, accessed August 30, 2025, https://history.churchofjesuschrist.org/chd/individual/levira-annette-clark-smith-1842.

13. Gaunt and Smith, "Samuel H. Smith: Faithful Brother of Joseph and Hyrum." Young, *A History of Round Prairie and Plymouth, 1831–1875*, 64–66, 87. David John Buerger, "The Development of the Mormon Temple Endowment Ceremony," *Dialogue: A Journal of Mormon Thought* 20, no. 4 (Winter 1987). Quinn, *Mormon Hierarchy: Origins of Power*, 176, 498. Smith, *Mary Smith*, 87.

14. Spencer W. McBride, "The Council of Fifty and Joseph Smith's Presidential Ambitions," in *The Council of Fifty: What the Records Reveal About Mormon History*, edited by Matthew J. Grow and R. Eric Smith (Deseret Book, 2017), 21–30. Derek R. Sainsbury, *Storming the Nation: The Unknown Contributions of Joseph Smith's Political Missionaries* (Deseret Book, 2020), https://rsc.byu.edu/storming-nation/prologue-joseph-smith-ran-president. *General Smith's Views of the Powers and Policy of the Government of the United States*, circa 26 January–7 February 1844, p. 1, Joseph Smith Papers, accessed April 6, 2025, https://www.josephsmithpapers.org/paper-summary/general-smiths-views-of-the-powers-and-policy-of-the-government-of-the-united-states-circa-26-january-7-february-1844/1. Arnold K Garn, "Joseph Smith for President: The Quorum of the Twelve Apostles in New England," in *Regional Studies of Latter-day Saint Church History: The New England States*, 47–64. "Church Magazines and Newspapers," The Church of Jesus Christ of Latter-day Saints, accessed August 30, 2025, https://history.churchofjesuschrist.org/training/library/featured-collections/church-magazines-and-newspapers.

15. Century of Black Mormons, J. Willard Marriott Library, Digital Exhibitions, accessed August 30, 2025, https://exhibits.lib.utah.edu/s/century-of-black-mormons/page/welcome.

16. Matthew L. Harris, *Second-Class Saints: Black Mormons and the Struggle for Racial Equality* (Oxford University Press, 2024), 1–27.

17. "Council of Fifty," The Church of Jesus Christ of Latter-day Saints, accessed August, 30, 2025, https://www.churchofjesuschrist.org/study/history/topics/

council-of-fifty. W. Paul Reeve, "The Council of Fifty and the Search for Religious Liberty," in *The Council of Fifty*, 181–90. D. Michael Quinn, "The Council of Fifty and Its Members, 1844–1945," *BYU Studies Quarterly* 20, issue. 2, article 4 (April 1, 1980): 163–97.

Chapter 35

1. Thomas Sharp ed., *Warsaw Signal* (Sharp & Head, June 12, 1844). Resolution, 10 June 1844, p. 1, Joseph Smith Papers, accessed April 7, 2025, https://www.josephsmithpapers.org/paper-summary/resolution-10-june-1844/1. Resignation from Samuel Smith, 23 May 1842, p. 1, Joseph Smith Papers, accessed April 7, 2025, https://www.josephsmithpapers.org/paper-summary/resignation-from-samuel-smith-23-may-1842/1. *Nauvoo Expositor*, vol. 1, no. 1, June 7, 1844, accessed August 30, 2025, https://www.josephsmithpapers.org/paper-summary/nauvoo-expositor-7-june-1844/1. "Freedom of the Press," Gene Policinski and Ken Paulson, "Freedom of the Press," Free Speech Center, accessed October 28, 2025, https://firstamendment.mtsu.edu/article/freedom-of-the-press/. Dallin H. Oaks, "Legally Suppressing the Nauvoo Expositor in 1844," in *Sustaining the Law: Joseph Smith's Legal Encounters*, ed. Gordon A. Madsen, et al. (BYU Studies, 2014), 427–59. Larry C. Porter, "The Brothers' Final Hours in Carthage," *Church News* (archive), 9 July 1994, https://www.thechurchnews.com/1994/7/9/23256843/the-brothers-final-hours-in-carthage/.

Chapter 36

1. Mary Bailey Smith Norman, letter to Sue Smith Beatty, October 21, 1915. Mary Bailey Smith Norman, "Samuel Harrison Smith (reminiscence)," 1914, in Joseph B. Smith Collection, 1834–1981, Church History Library. Kenneth W. Godfrey, "Remembering the Deaths of Joseph and Hyrum Smith," in *Joseph Smith: The Prophet, The Man*, ed. Susan Easton Black and Charles D. Tate Jr., (Religious Studies Center, Brigham Young University, 1993), 301–15. Kenneth W. Godfrey, "Correspondence Between William R. Hamilton and Samuel H. B. Smith Regarding the Martyrdom of Joseph and Hyrum Smith," *Nauvoo Journal* 11, no. 2 (Fall 1999): 83–92. Brian Reeves, "'A Battle Ensued.'" Dean Jarman, "The Life and Contributions of Samuel Harrison Smith" (Thesis, Brigham Young University, 1961), 102–03.
2. Norman, "Samuel Harrison Smith (reminiscence)."
3. Smith, *Revised and Enhanced History of Joseph Smith by His Mother*, 457. Gaunt and Smith, "Samuel H. Smith: Faithful Brother of Joseph and Hyrum." Richard Van Wagoner and Steven C. Walker, "The Joseph/Hyrum Smith Funeral Sermon," *BYU Studies Quarterly*, 23, issue. 1, article 2 (1983): 3–18. Susan Easton Black, "The Tomb of Joseph," in *The Disciple as Witness: Essays on Latter-day Saint History and Doctrine in Honor of Richard Lloyd Anderson*, ed. Stephen D. Ricks et al. (FARMS, 2000).
4. Gaunt and Smith, "Samuel H. Smith: Faithful Brother of Joseph and Hyrum."
5. Quinn, *Mormon Hierarchy*, 149–55, 205. Robert C. Fillerup, compiler, *William Clayton's Nauvoo Diaries and Personal Writings*, July 12, 1844. Smith, *The Revised and Enhanced History of Joseph Smith by His Mother*, 459.
6. Norman, "Samuel Harrison Smith (reminiscence)."
7. Gaunt and Smith, "Samuel H. Smith: Faithful Brother of Joseph and Hyrum."
8. Lachlan Mackay, "A Brief History of the Smith Family Nauvoo Cemetery," *Mormon Historical Studies* 3, no. 2 (Fall 2002): 240–52.

Chapter 37

1. Quinn, *Mormon Hierarchy*, 149–55. William Smith, "A Letter from William Smith," *New York Daily Tribune*, May 28, 1857. Richard Abanes, *One Nation Under Gods: A History of the Mormon Church* (Four Walls Eight Windows, 2002), 207. Bates, "William Smith, 1811–1893: Problematic Patriarch," 11–23.
2. Mormon Polygamy Documents, accessed August 30, 2025, 5, https://mormonpolygamydocuments.org/wp-content/uploads/2014/12/JSP_Book_70.pdf.
3. Quinn, *Mormon Hierarchy*, 384n52.
4. Walker, *United in Faith*, 236.
5. Asa Calkin, ed. and pub., *Journal of Discourses*, vol. 5 (1858): 77.
6. Quinn, *Mormon Hierarchy*, 155.
7. "Levira Clark," The Church of Jesus Christ of Latter-day Saints, Church History Biographical Database, https://history.churchofjesuschrist.org/chd/individual/levira-clark-1815. "Dustin Amy," The Church of Jesus Christ of Latter-day Saints, Church History Biographical Database, accessed August 30, 2025, https://history.churchofjesuschrist.org/chd/individual/dustin-amy-1801?lang=en. Andrew Jenson, *Latter-day Saint Biographical Encyclopedia*, vol. 3 (Andrew Jenson History Company and printed by the Arrow Press, 1920), 242–43. Lucy Mack Smith, History, 1845, p. 20, Joseph Smith Papers, accessed April 8, 2025, https://www.josephsmithpapers.org/paper-summary/lucy-mack-smith-history-1845/27#historical-intro. "Levira Annette Clark Smith," The Church of Jesus Christ of Latter-day Saints, Church History Biographical Database, accessed August 30, 2025, https://history.churchofjesuschrist.org/chd/individual/levira-annette-clark-smith-1842.
8. Newell and Avery, *Mormon Enigma*, 347n13.
9. Walker, *United in Faith* 244n110.
10. D. Michael Quinn, "The Mormon Succession Crisis of 1844," *BYU Studies Quarterly* 16, issue. 2, article 2 (April 1, 1976): 222–33. Michael Kennedy, "Financial Support of the Smith Family After the Murders of Joseph and Hyrum," Joseph Smith and Emma Hale Smith Historical Society, September 20, 2020, https://josephsmithjr.org/financial-support-of-the-smith-family-after-the-murders-of-joseph-hyrum/. Ronald K. Esplin, "Joseph, Brigham and the Twelve: A Succession of Continuity," *BYU Studies* 21, no. 3 (Summer 1981): 312–20.

Epilogue

1. Gaunt and Smith, "Samuel H. Smith: Faithful Brother of Joseph and Hyrum."
2. "Facts and Statistics," The Church of Jesus Christ of Latter-day Saints, Newsroom, accessed August 30, 2025, https://newsroom.churchofjesuschrist.org/facts-and-statistics. "Church Now Fourth Largest in the U.S," The Church of Jesus Christ of Latter-day Saints, accessed August 30, 2025, https://www.churchofjesuschrist.org/study/liahona/2005/08/news-of-the-church/church-now-fourth-largest-in-the-u-s-growth-continues-worldwide. "Temple List," The Church of Jesus Christ of Latter-day Saints, accessed August 30, 2025, https://www.churchofjesuschrist.org/temples/list?.
3. Community of Christ, accessed August 30, 2025, https://cofchrist.org/about-us/.
4. Thomas Burr, "Book of Mormon Touted as the Fourth Most Influential Work in American Literature," *Salt Lake Tribune*, December 8, 2016, https://archive.sltrib.com/article.php?id=4684387&itype=CMSID.
5. "The Book of Mormon Ranks as the Sixth Most Published Book in the World," *Moroni Channel*, April 5, 2023, https://www.moronichannel.org/newsroom/the-book-of-mormon-ranks-as-6th-most-published-book-in-the-world/.

SOURCES CITED

Abanes, Richard. *One Nation Under Gods: A History of the Mormon Church*. Four Walls Eight Windows, 2002.

Aichele, Gary J. "The Making of the Vermont Constitution: 1777–1824." *Vermont History: The Proceedings of the Vermont Historical Society* 56, no. 3 (Summer 1988): 137–90.

Allen County Public Library Genealogy Center. *History of Seneca Co. New York*. Everts, Ensign & Everts, 1876.

Allen, James B. "The Significance of Joseph Smith's 'First Vision' in Mormon Thought." *Dialogue: A Journal of Mormon Thought* 1, no. 3 (1966): 29–46.

Allen, James B. and Glen M. Leonard. *The Story of the Latter-day Saints*. Deseret Book, 1976. Reprint, 1992.

Anderson, Richard Lloyd. "Explaining Away the Book of Mormon Witnesses." FAIR. Accessed August 30, 2025. https://www.fairlatterdaysaints.org/conference/august-2004/explaining-away-the-book-of-mormon-witnesses.

Atack, Jeremy, Robert A. Margo, and Paul W. Rhode. "Industrialization and Urbanization in Nineteenth-Century America." *Regional Science and Urban Economics* 94 (May 2022). https://doi.org/10.1016/j.regsciurbeco.2021.103678.

Backman, Milton Vaughn and James B. Allen. "Membership of Certain of Joseph Smith's Family in the Western Presbyterian Church in Palmyra." *BYU Studies Quarterly* 10, issue 4, article 14 (October 10, 1970): 211–13, 482–84.

Barney, Ronald O. "Joseph Smith Goes to Washington." In *Joseph Smith, the Prophet and Seer*, edited by Richard Neitzel Holzapfel and Kent P. Jackson. Deseret Book, 2010.

Bates, Irene. "William Smith, 1811–1893: Problematic Patriarch." *Dialogue: A Journal of Mormon Thought* 16, no. 2 (Summer 1983): 11–23.

Baugh, Alexander L. "For Their Salvation Is Necessary and Essential to Our Salvation." In *An Eye of Faith: Essays in Honor of Richard O. Cowan*, edited by Kenneth L. Alford and Richard E. Bennett. BYU Religious Studies Center, 2015.

Becker, John E. *A History of the Village of Waterloo New York and Thesaurus of Related Facts*. Waterloo Library and Historical Society, 1949.

Bittner, Terrie Lynn. "Samuel H. Smith: Faithful Through Many Trials." History of Mormonism. Accessed August 30, 2025. https://historyofmormonism.com/2013/06/27/samuel-h-smith/.

Black, Susan Easton. "Reynolds Cahoon." Doctrine and Covenants Central. Accessed August 30, 2025. https://doctrineandcovenantscentral.org/people-of-the-dc/reynolds-cahoon/.

Black, Susan Easton. "The Tomb of Joseph." In *The Disciple as Witness: Essays on Latter-day Saint History and Doctrine in Honor of Richard Lloyd Anderson,* edited by Stephen D. Ricks, Donald W. Parry, and Andrew H. Hedges. FARMS, 2000.

Blair, Alma R. "The Haun's Mill Massacre." *BYU Studies Quarterly* 13, issue 1, article 8 (1973): 62–67. https://scholarsarchive.byu.edu/cgi/viewcontent.cgi?article=1564&context=byusq.

Boardman, Mark. "Battle for the Promised Land." *True West: History of the American Frontier,* July 4, 2019. https://truewestmagazine.com/article/battle-for-the-promised-land/.

Bourne, Jenny. "Slavery in the United States." Economic History Association. Accessed October 14, 2025. https://eh.net/encyclopedia/slavery-in-the-united-states/.

Brodie, Fawn M. *No Man Knows My History.* 2nd ed. Vintage Books, 1995.

Brown, S. Kent, et al. "The Joseph Smith Translation of the Bible: A Panel." In *Scriptures for the Modern World,* edited by Paul R. Cheesman and C. Wilfred Griggs. Religious Studies Center, Brigham Young University, 1984.

Brynn, Edward. "Patterns of Dissent: Opposition to the War of 1812." *Vermont History: Proceedings of the Vermont Historical Society* 40, no. 1 (Winter 1972): 10–27.

Buerger, David John. "The Development of the Mormon Temple Endowment Ceremony." *Dialogue: A Journal of Mormon Thought* 20, no. 4 (Winter 1987): 75–122.

Burns, James MacGregor. *Fire and Light: How the Enlightenment Transformed Our World.* Thomas Dunne Books, St. Martin's Griffin, 2013.

Burr, Thomas. "Book of Mormon Touted as the Fourth Most Influential Work in American Literature." *Salt Lake Tribune,* December 8, 2016. https://archive.sltrib.com/article.php?id=4684387&itype=CMSID.

Bushman, Richard Lyman. *Joseph Smith: Rough Stone Rolling.* Knopf, 2005.

Bushnell, Mark. "Then Again: Vermonters Were Bitterly Divided over the War of 1812." *vtdigger,* October 17, 2021. https://vtdigger.org/2021/10/17/then-again-vermonters-were-bitterly-divided-over-the-war-of-1812/.

Bustard, Bruce I. "Spirited Republic." *Prologue,* Winter 2014, 15–22. https://www.archives.gov/files/publications/prologue/2014/winter/spirited.pdf.

Caldwell County Commission. "The History of Caldwell County." Accessed August 30, 2025. https://www.caldwellco.missouri.org/about-and-history-of-caldwell-county/.

Calkin, Asa, ed. and pub. *Journal of Discourses,* vol. 5. 1858.

Cannon, Donald Q., ed. "Joseph Smith." In *Latter-day Prophets and the United States Constitution.* Religious Studies Center, Brigham Young University, 1991.

Chapin, William. *A Complete Reference Gazetteer of the United States of North America; Containing a General View of the United States.* W. Chapin and J. B. Taylor, 1839.

Child, Hamilton. *Gazetteer of Orange County Vt. 1762–1888, History of the Town of Tunbridge, Syracuse, N.Y.* The Syracuse Journal Company, Printers and Binders, 1888.

The Church of Jesus Christ of Latter-day Saints. "Church Magazines and Newspapers." Accessed August 30, 2025. https://history.churchofjesuschrist.org/training/library/featured-collections/church-magazines-and-newspapers.

The Church of Jesus Christ of Latter-day Saints. "The Church Moves to Northern Missouri." Accessed August 30, 2025. https://www.churchofjesuschrist.org/study/manual/doctrine-and-covenants-and-church-history-seminary-teacher-manual-2014/section-6/lesson-121-the-church-moves-to-northern-missouri.

The Church of Jesus Christ of Latter-day Saints. "Church Now Fourth Largest in the U.S." Accessed August 30, 2025. https://www.churchofjesuschrist.org/study/liahona2005/08/news-of-the-church/church-now-fourth-largest-in-the-u-s-growth-continues-worldwide.

The Church of Jesus Christ of Latter-day Saints. "Council of Fifty." Accessed August 30, 2025. https://www.churchofjesuschrist.org/study/history/topics/council-of-fifty.

The Church of Jesus Christ of Latter-day Saints. "Danites." Accessed August 30, 2025. https://www.churchofjesuschrist.org/study/history/topics/danites.

The Church of Jesus Christ of Latter-day Saints. "Dustin Amy." Church History Biographical Database. Accessed August 30, 2025. https://history.churchofjesuschrist.org/chd/individual/dustin-amy-1801.

The Church of Jesus Christ of Latter-day Saints. "Facts and Statistics." Newsroom. Accessed October 21, 2025. https://newsroom.churchofjesuschrist.org/facts-and-statistics.

The Church of Jesus Christ of Latter-day Saints. "Family of Joseph Smith Sr. and Lucy Mack Smith: The First Family of the Restoration." *Ensign.* December 2005.

The Church of Jesus Christ of Latter-day Saints. "Free People of Color." *Evening and Morning Star*, vol. 1–2, 2005, 218. https://contentdm.lib.byu.edu/digital/collection/NCMP1820-1846/id/28024.

The Church of Jesus Christ of Latter-day Saints. "Growing Conflict in Illinois." Accessed October 28, 2025. https://www.churchofjesuschrist.org/study/manual/church-history-in-the-fulness-of-times/chapter-twenty-one.

The Church of Jesus Christ of Latter-day Saints. Joseph Smith Papers. Church History Department. www.josephsmithpapers.org.

The Church of Jesus Christ of Latter-day Saints. "Levira Annette Clark Smith." Church History Biographical Database. Accessed August 30, 2025. https://history.churchofjesuschrist.org/chd/individual/levira-annette-clark-smith-1842.

The Church of Jesus Christ of Latter-day Saints. "Levira Clark." Church History Biographical Database. Accessed August 30, 2025. https://history.churchofjesuschrist.org/chd/individual/levira-clark-1815.

The Church of Jesus Christ of Latter-day Saints. *Millennial Star*, Nov. 26, 1864, 774.

The Church of Jesus Christ of Latter-day Saints. "Missions of Samuel H. Smith." *Ensign*, August 2008, 48. https://www.churchofjesuschrist.org/study/ensign/2008/08/samuel-h-smith-faithful-brother-of-joseph-and-hyrum/the-missions-of-samuel-h-smith.

The Church of Jesus Christ of Latter-day Saints. "Temple List." Accessed August 30, 2025. https://www.churchofjesuschrist.org/temples/list.

The Church of Jesus Christ of Latter-day Saints. "Zion's Camp (Camp of Israel)." Accessed August 30, 2025. https://www.churchofjesuschrist.org/study/history/topics/zions-camp-camp-of-israel.

Clark, Linda Darus. "Lewis & Clark Expedition." National Archives. Accessed August 30, 2025. https://www.archives.gov/education/lessons/lewis-clark#background.

Clarke, S. J. *History of McDonough County Illinois, Its Cities, Towns, and Villages with Early Reminiscences, Personal Incidents and Anecdotes.* D. W. Lusk, State Printer and Binder, 1878.

Community of Christ. Accessed August 30, 2025. https://cofchrist.org/about-us/.

De Groote, Michael. "How Gold Were the Golden Plates?" *Deseret News*, July 7, 2010.

Dickinson, Ellen E. *New Light on Mormonism.* Funk & Wagnalls, 1885.

Digital History. "Growth of Cities." Accessed August 30, 2025. https://www.digitalhistory.uh.edu/disp_textbook.cfm?smtID=2&psid=3514.

Divett, Robert T. "Medicine and the Mormons: A Historical Perspective." *Dialogue: A Journal of Mormon Thought* 12, no. 3 (Fall 1979): 16–25.

Dunn, Elizabeth. "5 19th-Century Utopian Communities in the United States." *History. com*, January 22, 2013. Accessed August 30, 2025. https://www.history.com/articles/5-19th-century-utopian-communities-in-the-united-states.

Enders, Donald L. "The Joseph Smith, Sr., Family: Farmers of the Genesee." In *Joseph Smith: The Prophet, The Man*, edited by Susan Easton Black and Charles D. Tate Jr. Religious Studies Center, Brigham Young University, 1993.

Esplin, Ronald K. "Joseph, Brigham and the Twelve: A Succession of Continuity." *BYU Studies* 21, no. 3 (Summer 1981): 312–320.

FAIR. "Joseph Smith/Polygamy/Cochranites." Accessed August 30, 2025. https://www.fairlatterdaysaints.org/answers/Joseph_Smith/Polygamy/Cochranites.

FamilySearch. "Hyrum Smith." Accessed August 30, 2025. https://ancestors.familysearch.org/en/KWJT-6XJ/hyrum-smith-1800-1844.

FamilySearch. "Mary Bailey Smith." Accessed August 30, 2025. https://ancestors.familysearch.org/en/L21G-6BL/mary-bailey-smith-1837-1916.

Fillerup, Robert C., compiler. *William Clayton's Nauvoo Diaries and Personal Writings.* July 12, 1844.

Finke, Roger and Rodney Stark. "Turning Pews into People: Estimating 19th Century Church Membership." *Journal for the Scientific Study of Religion* 25, no. 2 (June 1986): 180–92.

Flake, Lawrence R. *Prophets and Apostles of the Last Dispensation.* Religious Studies Center, Brigham Young University, 2001.

Garr, Arnold K. "Joseph Smith for President: The Quorum of the Twelve Apostles in New England." In *Regional Studies of Latter-day Saint Church History: The New England States*, edited by Donald Q. Cannon and Garr. Religious Studies Center, Brigham Young University, 2004.

Gaunt, LaRene Porter and Robert A. Smith. "Samuel H. Smith: Faithful Brother of Joseph and Hyrum." *Ensign*, August 2008, 44–51. https://www.churchofjesuschrist.org/study/ensign/2008/08/samuel-h-smith-faithful-brother-of-joseph-and-hyrum.

Godfrey, Kenneth W. "Correspondence Between William R. Hamilton and Samuel H. B. Smith Regarding the Martyrdom of Joseph and Hyrum Smith." *Nauvoo Journal* 11, no. 2 (Fall 1999): 83–92.

Godfrey, Kenneth W. "Remembering the Deaths of Joseph and Hyrum Smith." In *Joseph Smith: The Prophet, The Man*, edited by Susan Easton Black and Charles D. Tate Jr. Religious Studies Center, Brigham Young University, 1993.

Godfrey, Matthew C. "A Great Blessing: The Calling of the Original Twelve Apostles in This Dispensation." The Church of Jesus Christ of Latter-day Saints. https://history.churchofjesuschrist.org/content/perspectives-on-church-history/a-great-blessing.

Gordon, Thomas F. *Gazetteer of the State of New York: Comprehending Its Colonial History*. Published by the author, 1836.

Hales, Brian C. *Joseph Smith's Polygamy*, vol. 2: *History*. Greg Kofford Books, 2013.

Hales, Brian C. "Joseph Smith's Practice of Plural Marriage." BYU Religious Studies Center. Accessed October 22, 2025. https://rsc.byu.edu/sites/default/files/pub_content/pdf/Joseph_Smiths_Practice_of_Plural_Marraige.pdf

Harper, Kimberly. "Alexander W. Doniphan." Historic Missourians. Accessed August 30, 2025. https://historicmissourians.shsmo.org/alexander-doniphan/.

Harper, Steven C. "The Eleven Witnesses." In *The Coming Forth of the Book of Mormon: A Marvelous Work and a Wonder*, edited by Dannis L. Largey, et al. Deseret Book, 2015.

Harris, Matthew L. *Second-Class Saints: Black Mormons and the Struggle for Racial Equality*. Oxford University Press, 2024.

Hartog, Hendrik. "Marital Exits and Marital Expectations in Nineteenth Century America." Philip A. Hart Memorial Lecture, Georgetown University Law Center, April 10, 1991. https://scholarship.law.georgetown.edu/hartlecture/8/.

Harvard Business School. "1837: The Hard Times." Accessed August 30, 2025. https://www.library.hbs.edu/hc/crises/1837.html.

Haws, J. B. "The Lost 116 Pages Story." In *The Coming Forth of the Book of Mormon: A Marvelous Work and a Wonder*, edited by Dennis L. Largey, et al. Deseret Book, 2015.

History.com. "Louisiana Purchase." Accessed August 30, 2025. https://www.history.com/topics/19th-century/louisiana-purchase.

History.com. "Monroe Doctrine." Accessed August 30, 2025. https://www.history.com/topics/19th-century/monroe-doctrine.

Hoffman, Alexander Von and John Felkner. "The Historical Origins and Causes of Urban Decentralization in the United States." Joint Center for Housing Studies, Harvard University, 2002. https://www.jchs.harvard.edu/sites/default/files/von_hoffman_w02-1.pdf.

Howe, E. D. *Mormonism Unvailed: Or, a Faithful Account of That Singular Imposition and Delusion, from Its Rise to the Present Time*. Published by the author, 1834.

Hyde, Orson. Orson Hyde Journal, 1832 February -December, Typescript of Journal. Church History Library (The Church of Jesus Christ of Latter-day Saints).

Ivie, Evan L. and Douglas C. Heiner. "Deaths in Early Nauvoo, Illinois, 1839–1846, and in Winter Quarters, Nebraska, 1846–48." *Religious Educator* 10, no. 3 (2009): 63–174.

Jarman, Dean. "The Life and Contributions of Samuel Harrison Smith." Thesis, Brigham Young University, 1961.

Jenson, Andrew. *Encyclopedic History of The Church of Jesus Christ of Latter-day Saints*. Deseret News Publishing Company, 1941.

Jenson, Andrew. *Latter-day Saint Biographical Encyclopedia*, vol 3. Andrew Jenson History Company and printed by the Arrow Press, 1920.

Joseph Smith Foundation. "Ancestry of the Prophet Joseph Smith." Accessed August 30, 2025. https://josephsmithfoundation.org/ancestry-of-the-prophet-joseph-smith/.

Joseph Smith Sr. and Lucy Mack Smith Family Organization. "The Early Mack Family in Gilsum, NH." Accessed August 30, 2025. https://josephsmithsr.org/wp-content/uploads/2023/10/Mack-Family-in-Gilsum.pdf.

Juvenile Instructor (blog). "A Son of the Forest and an Intelligent Son of Abraham: Orson Hyde and Samuel Smith Meet William Apess, 1832." November 21, 2013. https://juvenileinstructor.org/a-son-of-the-forest-and-an-intelligent-son-of-abraham-william-hyde-and-samuel-smith-meet-william-apess-1832/.

Kennedy, Michael. "Financial Support of the Smith Family After the Murders of Joseph and Hyrum." Joseph Smith and Emma Hale Smith Historical Society, September 20, 2020. https://josephsmithjr.org/financial-support-of-the-smith-family-after-the-murders-of-joseph-hyrum/.

Kettley, Marlene C., Arnold K. Garr, and Craig K. Manscill. *Mormon Thoroughfare: A History of the Church in Illinois, 1830–1839*. Religious Studies Center, Brigham Young University, 2006.

Kidd, Thomas S. *America's Religious History: Faith, Politics, and the Shaping of a Nation*. Zondervan Academic, 2019.

Latter Day Light. "Samuel Harrison Smith." Accessed August 30, 2025. https://latterdaylight.com/samuel-harrison-smith/.

Lebergott, Stanley. "Labor Force and Employment, 1800–1960." In *Output, Employment, and Productivity in the United States After 1800*, edited by Dorothy S. Brady National Bureau of Economic Research, 1966. https://www.nber.org/system/files/chapters/c1567/c1567.pdf.

Library of Congress. "Rural Life in the Late 19th Century." Accessed August 30, 2025. https://www.loc.gov/classroom-materials/united-states-history-primary-source-timeline/rise-of-industrial-america-1876-1900/rural-life-in-late-19th-century/.

Lightner, Mary E. Rollins. "Ran from the Mob." *Deseret Evening News*. February 20, 1904, 24.

Mackay, Lachlan. "A Brief History of the Smith Family Nauvoo Cemetery." *Mormon Historical Studies* 3, no. 2 (Fall 2002): 240–52.

Macomb Area Chamber of Commerce. "History of Macomb." Accessed by August 30, 2025. https://www.macombareachamber.com/history-of-macomb/.

Madesen, Gordan A. "Joseph Smith's 1826 Trial: The Legal Setting." *BYU Studies Quarterly* 30, issue. 2, article 7 (April 1, 1990): 91–108.

Maine Historical Society. "The Cochran Fanaticism in York County." *Maine History* 20, issue 1 (1980): 23–39. https://digitalcommons.library.umaine.edu/mainehistoryjournal/vol20/iss1/3.

McBride, Spencer W. "The Council of Fifty and Joseph Smith's Presidential Ambitions." In *The Council of Fifty: What the Records Reveal About Mormon History*, edited by Matthew J. Grow, et al. Deseret Book, 2017.

McBride, Spencer W. and Jennifer Hull Dorsey, eds. *New York's Burned-Over District: A Documentary History*. Cornell University Press, 2023.

Metcalfe, Erin B. "Firm and Steadfast in the Faith." *Mormon Historical Studies*, 14, no. 2 (Fall 2013): 109–21.

Morgan, Meghan Hamilton. "A Brief History of Conscription 1812–2002." Chancellor's Honors Program Projects, TRACE: Tennessee Research and Creative Exchange, Spring 5-2002. https://trace.tennessee.edu/utk_chanhonoproj/580.

Morley, Richard Henrie. "The Life and Contributions of Isaac Morley." Thesis, Brigham Young University, 1965.

Moroni Channel. "The Book of Mormon Ranks as the Sixth Most Published Book in the World." Accessed August 30, 2025. https://www.moronichannel.org/newsroom/the-book-of-mormon-ranks-as-6th-most-published-book-in-the-world/.

Mormon Polygamy Documents. Accessed August 30, 2025. https://mormonpolygamy documents.org/wp-content/uploads/2014/12/JSP_Book_70.pdf.

Morris, Larry E. "Empirical Witnesses of the Gold Plates." *Dialogue: A Journal of Mormon Thought* 52, no. 2 (Summer 2019): 59–84.

National Constitution Center. "The Louisiana Purchase: Jefferson's Constitutional Gamble." Accessed August 30, 2025. https://constitutioncenter.org/blog/the-louisiana-purchase-jeffersons-constitutional-gamble.

National Geographic. "The Indian Removal Act and the Trail of Tears." Accessed August 30, 2025. https://education.nationalgeographic.org/resource/indian-removal-act-and-trail-tears/.

National Geographic Society. "Voting Rights Throughout United States History." Accessed August 30, 2025. https://web.archive.org/web/20220703214302/ttps://education.nationalgeographic.org/resource/voting-rights-throughout-history/.

Nauvoo Expositor. vol. 1, no. 1 (June 7, 1844).

Newell, Linda King and Valeen Tippetts Avery. *Mormon Enigma: Emma Hale Smith.* Doubleday & Company, 1984.

Nielsen, Chad. "The Smith Family and the First Vision." *Times and Seasons.* June 25, 2022.

http://archive.timesandseasons.org/2022/06/the-smith-family-and-the-first-vision/index.html.

Norman, Mary Bailey Smith. Letter to Sue Smith Beatty. October 21, 1915. Harold B. Lee Library. Brigham Young University.

Norman, Mary Bailey Smith. "Samuel Harrison Smith (reminiscence), 1914." In Joseph B. Smith Collection, 1834–1981. Church History Library.

Oaks, Dallin H. "Legally Suppressing the Nauvoo Expositor in 1844." In *Sustaining the Law: Joseph Smith's Legal Encounters*, edited by Gordon A. Madsen, Jeffrey N. Walker, and John W. Welch. BYU Studies, 2014.

Olmstead, Jacob W. "Life on the Smith Farm." The Church of Jesus Christ of Latter-day Saints. February 22, 2019. https://history.churchofjesuschrist.org/content/historic-sites/palmyra/life-on-the-smith-farm.

Peterson, J. W. "Another Testimony, Statement of William Smith, Concerning Joseph the Prophet." *Deseret Evening News*, January 20, 1894, 11.

Platt, Lyman D. "Members of The Church of Jesus Christ of Latter-day Saints Baptized by September 26, 1830." Ensign Peak Foundation. https://ensignpeakfoundation.org/wp-content/uploads/2013/05/NJ1_Platt4.pdf.

Policinski, Gene and Ken Paulson. "Freedom of the Press." Free Speech Center. Accessed October 28, 2025. https://firstamendment.mtsu.edu/article/freedom-of-the-press/.

Ponzetti, Nancy. "The Cochrane Craze." *BHHS Newsletter*, Fall 2020. https://bhhsnewsletter.weebly.com/the-cochrane-craze.html.

Porter, Larry C. "The Brothers' Final Hours in Carthage." *Church News* (archive), July 9, 1994. https://www.thechurchnews.com/1994/7/9/23256843/the-brothers-final-hours-in-carthage/.

Porter, Larry C. *A Study of the Origins of The Church of Jesus Christ Latter-day Saints in the States of New York and Pennsylvania*. BYU Studies, 2000.

Quinn, D. Michael. "The Council of Fifty and Its Members, 1844–1945." *BYU Studies Quarterly* 20, issue 2, article 4 (April 1, 1980): 163–97.

Quinn, D. Michael. *Early Mormonism and the Magic World View*. Rev. ed. Signature Books, 1998. E-book.

Quinn, D. Michael. *The Mormon Hierarchy: Origins of Power*. Signature Books in association with Smith Research Associates, 1994.

Quinn, D. Michael. "The Mormon Succession Crisis of 1844." *BYU Studies Quarterly* 16, issue. 2, article 2 (April 1, 1976): 222–33.

Ray County Museum. "Battle of Crooked River." Accessed August 30, 2025. https://raycountymuseum.org/home/history/battle-of-crooked-river/.

Reeve, W. Paul. "The Council of Fifty and the Search for Religious Liberty." In *The Council of Fifty: What the Records Reveal About Mormon History*, edited by Matthew J. Grow and R. Eric Smith. Deseret Book, 2017.

Reeves, Brian. "'A Battle Ensued': John P. Greene and Samuel H. Smith in the Early Restoration." Accessed August 30, 2025. http://young.parkinsonfamily.org/john/histories/jpg-samuel-smith.htm.

Riney-Kehrberg, Pamela. "Farm Boys." Iowa State University Digital Repository. Accessed August 30, 2025. https://dr.lib.iastate.edu/server/api/core/bitstreams/ec1227bc-2fc6-471e-94a9-3024dbdd5e3a/content.

Rogers, Brent M. "Vienna Jaques: Woman of Faith." *Ensign*, June 2016. https://www.churchofjesuschrist.org/study/ensign/2016/06/vienna-jaques-woman-of-faith.

Russell, William D. "Investigating the Investigation." Review of *Investigating the Book of Mormon Witnesses*, by Richard Lloyd Anderson. *Dialogue: A Journal of Mormon Thought* 16, no. 2, (Summer 1983): 130–32.

Sainsbury, Derek R. *Storming the Nation: The Unknown Contributions of Joseph Smith's Political Missionaries.* Deseret Book, 2020. https://rsc.byu.edu/storming-nation/prologue-joseph-smith-ran-president.

Sharp, Thomas, editor. *Warsaw Signal.* Sharp & Head, June 12, 1844.

Shipps, Jan, and John W. Welch, eds. *The Journals of William E. McLellin, 1831–1836.* BYU Studies and University of Illinois of Press, 1994.

Shurtleff, Stella Cahoon. *Reynolds Cahoon and His Stalwart Sons: Utah Pioneers.* Paragon Press, 1960.

Smith, Lucy M., et al. *The Revised and Enhanced History of Joseph Smith by His Mother,* edited by Scot Facer Proctor and Maurine Jenson Proctor. Bookcraft, 1996.

Smith, Mary Bailey. Letter to Emma, December 23, 1834. Joseph B. Smith Jr. Collection. Church History Library.

Smith, Mary Bailey. Letter to Samuel, undated. Joseph B. Smith Jr. Collection. Church History Library.

Smith, Ruby K. *Mary Bailey,* Deseret Book, 1954.

Smith, Samuel Harrison. Diary, 1832 February–1833 May, Typescript of Diary. Church History Library.

Smith, William. "A Letter from William Smith." *New York Daily Tribune,* May 28, 1857, 5.

Smith, William. *William Smith on Mormonism: A True Account of the Origin of the Book of Mormon.* Herald Steam Book and Job Office, 1883.

Smith Sr., Joseph. "Patriarchal Blessings by Joseph Smith Sr." December 9, 1834. Accessed August 30, 2025. https://user.xmission.com/~research/mormonpdf/blessingsbyjssr.pdf.

Smithsonian American Art Museum. "The Age of the Common Man." Accessed August 30, 2025. https://americanexperience.si.edu/historical-eras/colonization-revolution-and-new-nation/pair-daniel-lamotte-independence-squire-jack-porter/.

Stahle, Shaun D. "Samuel H. Smith Honored by Family." *Church News* (archive), June 18, 2005. https://www.thechurchnews.com/2005/6/18/23236436/samuel-h-smith-honored-by-family/.

Students of History. "The War of 1812. Accessed August 30, 2025. https://www.studentsofhistory.com/war-of-1812-Timeline.

Sweeney, John Jr. "Biography of Samuel H. Smith to 1840." Thesis, Brigham Young University, 1972.

SUNY OER Services. "United States Population Chart." Accessed August 30, 2025. https://courses.lumenlearning.com/suny-ushistory1ay/chapter/united-states-population-chart/.

Taylor, Don B. and Richard Bennett. "Samuel Harrison Smith, a Prophet's Brother." *Journal of Undergraduate Research* 2014, issue 1, article 1317. https://scholarsarchive.byu.edu/jur/vol2014/iss1/1317/.

Tunbridge Town Plan. Tunbridge Planning Commission, December 10, 2020. https://tunbridgevt.org/wp-content/uploads/2021/01/Tunbridge-Transmittal-Draft-w-maps-2020.pdf.

Tyler, Daniel. "Incidents of Experience." In *Scraps of Biography: Tenth Book of the Faith-Promoting Series*. Juvenile Instructor Office, 1883.

University of Utah, J. Willard Marriott Library Digital Exhibitions. Century of Black Mormons. Accessed August 30, 2025. https://exhibits.lib.utah.edu/s/century-of-black-mormons/page/welcome.

Van Wagoner, Richard and Steven C. Walker. "The Joseph/Hyrum Smith Funeral Sermon." *BYU Studies Quarterly* 23, issue 1, article 2 (1983): 3–18.

Van Wagoner, Richard S. "Mormon Polyandry in Nauvoo." *Dialogue: Journal of Mormon Thought* 18, no. 3 (Fall 1985): 67–83.

Van Wagoner, Richard S. *Natural Born Seer: Joseph Smith, American Prophet, 1805–1830*. Smith Pettit Foundation, 2016.

Vermont Department of Environmental Conservation. "White River Watershed Water Quality and Aquatic Habitat Assessment Report." November 2012. https://dec.vermont.gov/sites/dec/files/documents/WSMD_mapp_basin9white_assessrpt_nov2012.pdf.

Vermont Fish & Wildlife Department. "Mammals." Accessed August 30, 2025. https://vtfishandwildlife.com/learn-more/vermont-critters/mammals.

Vermont Fish & Wildlife Department. "White River Streambank Management Area." Accessed August 30, 2025. https://vtfishandwildlife.com/sites/fishandwildlife/files/documents/Fish/SMA-maps/WhiteRiverSMA_Final.pdf.

Villars, Thomas. "Tunbridge Vermont State Soil." Accessed August 30, 2025. https://www.soils4teachers.org/files/s4t/k12outreach/vt-state-soil-booklet.pdf.

Vogel, Dan, ed. *Early Mormon Documents*. Vol. 2. Signature Books, 1998.

VT Open Geodata Portal. "Historical Census Municipal Population Counts 1791–2020." Accessed August 30, 2025. https://geodata.vermont.gov/datasets/84a286c51ece48488273710e1f49834e/explore.

Walker, Jeffrey, N. "The Kirtland Safety Society and the Fraud of Grandison Newell: A Legal Examination." *BYU Studies Quarterly* 54, issue 3, article 5 (2015): 33–148.

Walker, Kyle R. *United by Faith: The Joseph Sr. and Lucy Mack Smith Family*. Covenant Communications, 2005.

White River Tactical Basin Plan. Vermont Agency of Natural Resources. July 2013. https://dec.vermont.gov/sites/dec/files/wsm/mapp/docs/pl_WhiteRiverTacticalPlan.pdf.

Widtsoe, John A. *Joseph Smith: Seeker After Truth, Prophet of God*. Deseret News Press, 1951.

Willers, Diedrich, *Centennial Historical Sketch of the Town of Fayette, Seneca County, New York*. Press of W. F. Humphrey, 1900.

Wood, Wilford C. *Joseph Smith Begins His Work*. Vol 2. Wilford C. Wood Publisher, 1962.

Wright, Dennis A., and Geoffrey A. Wright. "The New England Common School Experience of Joseph Smith Jr., 1810–16." In *Regional Studies of Latter-day Saint Church History: The New England States*, edited by Donald Q. Cannon and Arnold K. Garr. Religious Studies Center, Brigham Young University, 2004.

Young, E. H. *A History of Round Prairie and Plymouth, 1831–1875*. Geo. J. Titus, Book and Job Printer, 1876.

Young, Phineas. "Phineas Young's Account of Receiving Book of Mormon from Samuel Smith." *Church News* (archive), February 24, 2001. https://www.thechurchnews .com/2001/2/24/23244824/phineas-youngs-account-of-receiving-book-of-mormon-from-samuel-smith/.

INDEX